Published by:
LiveLearnAndProsper.com
3123 S. Semoran Blvd., Suite 289
Orlando, FL 32822

Visit us on the web at http://www.LiveLearnAndProsper.com
E-Mail: JohnRoberts@LiveLearnAndProsper.com

5th printing—Rel 53v31—9/23/13

Table Of Contents

Table Of Contents

Part 1: Beginnings: My Wakeup Call In 1987

I got my first investment wakeup call on Black Monday, October 19, 1987.

The stock market crashed 22%.

I was a typical company employee back then, managing Corporate IT for the second largest retail department store in the United States, and heavily invested in my company's stock — and not much else.

I watched helplessly as my stock portfolio dwindled in front of my eyes

I watched helplessly as my stock portfolio, consisting of just one stock, dwindled in front of my eyes. Does this story have a familiar sound to you? I was, perhaps, an investor just like you.

Fortunately, the market recovered, with some mutual funds actually getting back to even by the end of the year. And I breathed a sigh of relief.

You might think I made some big changes after that scare. But I didn't. I changed nothing about my investing portfolio—that is to say, my one and only stock.

Looking back, the list of investing mistakes I was making was rather lengthy. Like having all my eggs in one basket, no plan to minimize losses, poor research, on and on, little things like that.

And although the solutions are obvious today, I wouldn't have known much what to do back then, even if I'd tried.

Part 1: Beginnings: The Last Crash — But With A Difference

Fast forward to 2008 as the housing bubble went bust, the stock market came unglued, and millions of investors watched in horror as their stocks plummeted — and their hopes and dreams went up in smoke. Looking at a key market index of that period, stocks fell a whopping 38%. But many investors did far worse, losing half or more of their value.

As they were driving home after work, many investors had lost multiple times their days wages

There were days when these typical investors walked into their workplace, at least those fortunate enough to have jobs, and during their workday, the S&P 500 dropped 400 points. Which, said another way, goes like this. As they were driving home after that hard days work, many had lost multiple times their days wages in their investment portfolio.

What's that phrase, "not bad for a days work?" Let's revise that to "real bad for a days work."

Virtually everyone was affected, and I'm not here to tell you I ran the 2008 gauntlet unscathed. So why should you listen to me?

Because by that time, twenty-one years later, I was a far different kind of investor. Unrecognizable, actually, from that hapless chap back then on Black Monday, 1987.

I wasn't part of the audience at the boxing match this time around. I was fighting in the ring. I was proactively minimizing my losses, thus preserving and raising cash, which I could then invest in well researched stocks that were selling at ridiculously low firehouse sale prices.

The crash of 2008 presented incredible opportunities for those who knew how to seize them. So it was during these dark days that I made some of my best investments ever and ultimately increased the value of my portfolio by 2 1/2 times.

It was a far cry from the last go around. I wasn't the same 98 pound weakling getting stock market sand kicked in my face at the beach.

Here's an example of one of those opportunities I seized on in those dark days — a stock — which I'm going to reveal to

Part 1: Beginnings: The Last Crash — But With A Difference

you in a minute, so you can go check my facts for yourself. This stock tripled in value in eight months — going from $10 to $30 a share.

Here's what that means to you. Had you invested $10,000 in this company, your investment would have been worth $30,000 just eight months later. But it gets better.

I bought in at $13 a share. And because of that low price, it was paying me a 20% annual dividend. It's still paying me that dividend today. And at that dividend rate, you will double your money in just five years — on the dividends alone — without the stock ever going up.

But like I said, it did go up, and has gone up even more since then. Your original investment of $10,000 would be worth $50,000 as of this writing. Plus, add in three years of annual dividends of $6000 for $56,000 in three years. That's what I call "not bad for a days work."

I promised you the stock name, so here it is. The stock is called Mark West Energy Partners—symbol MWE. Go check it out (or you can just look at the chart below). This is what investment success looks like.

This is what investment success looks like

Now if you buy in at today's prices, don't be disappointed when you see the dividend is more like 5% — which is still quite good.

There are incredible opportunities out there when everyone else is heading for the hills

It just illustrates the point that there are incredible opportunities out there if you know how and when to buy low when everyone else is heading for the hills.

So MarkWest Energy Partners keeps paying me that fabulous dividend like clockwork. And it probably won't surprise you that I still own the stock as of this writing.

Part 1: Beginnings: So How Did I Do It?

So how did I, that hapless employee back in 1987, know how to do all that in 2008? What changed? Who am I, and what made such a big difference twenty-one years later — which, of course, is what makes this book so different too.

There are hundreds of books and experts promising to help you with stocks and investing

That's important to know because, after all, there are hundreds of books and experts out there promising to help you with stock investing. I just read a pretty good one myself recently, written by a popular investment TV personality entitled *Getting Back To Even*. In normal times, that would be considered a pretty low goal. But these are not normal times.

So just who the heck am I to teach you?

So just who the heck am I to teach you about stock investing?

Well, I am not a TV personality or a billionaire. I am not a Wall Street insider or giant hedge fund founder. And I am certainly not Warren Buffett — although I refer to him quite often.

I am just like you — somebody who woke up one day and realized if I was going to make money investing, I'd better get on with learning how to do it. So I did just that — and you can see what I learned works pretty well.

I'm not saying I'm some miracle worker—or hit these great returns every time ...

Now I'm not saying I'm some miracle worker or that I hit this return every time (although I discuss one much better than that in the book—try 1400% on for size — I tell you that stock name too), or that I always make money when markets are crashing — or that you will too.

... although I discuss one even better later in the book—try 1400% return on for size — I tell you that stock name too

And I'm not saying this is some foolproof system that removes all effort and thought from the process — although I have reduced these a great deal for you.

But you see, part of my background virtually assured I would figure this out and reduce the thought and effort down to the bare essentials.

Here's why. I've been a systems man for most of my career, i.e. simplifying processes, and I've gained quite a reputation for simplifying, and explaining, complex things.

And I take my research seriously. So, you remember when I

said I was just like you, that I realized that to make money investing, I'd better get on with learning how to do it?

I read book after book on stocks and investing, even during my vacations on my sailboat in Florida

Well, when I get my mind set on something, I'm an "all in" kind of guy. So when I finally woke up and realized I had all my eggs in my employer's stock basket, I started doing some serious investment research. I mean, even on vacation, I would spend days onboard my sailboat, the *Saline Solution II*, on Key Biscayne, Florida, reading book after book on stocks, commodities, futures, options, and market indexes.

I eventually became a Financial Consultant and stockbroker licensed with the New York Stock Exchange—with an office in beautiful downtown Coral Gables, Florida

But even that didn't satisfy me. So I studied many more months, sat for the New York Stock Exchange Series 7 exam and became a Financial Consultant and licensed stockbroker. I had an office in beautiful downtown Coral Gables, Florida where I helped my clients invest their personal money.

Ultimately I left the business, and am no longer licensed or associated with a broker/dealer, because I was offered a computer systems consulting job just too good to turn down. It involved creating computer disaster recovery procedures for hospitals — I told you I'm a systems man — and how appropriate is that—the disaster recovery part, I mean — when you think about the stock market?

So here I am again, an investor just like you. But I think you take my point that I went all in and developed some expertise along the way. I learned how to greatly improve my odds of success,.

And if you're interested, yours too.

Part 1: Beginnings: You Can Do It Too

So if I can do this, I think you can too. That's true for two reasons.

Nobody cares more about your money than you do

First off, nobody cares more about your money than you do. So you are motivated and you have your best interest at heart.

And second, many of the professionals simply aren't all they're cracked up to be. For example, most mutual fund managers can't beat the index of the S&P 500. And some studies have shown that you can throw darts at stock picks and do just as well as many professional investors.

Remember, amateurs built the Ark and professionals built the Titanic ...

... so you can do this

And here's another little insider tidbit for you to consider ... the minimum passing score on the New York Stock Exchange Stockbroker Series 7 exam is 70. Can you guess what the average stockbroker score is? It's 74, which says these "professionals" just barely passed (and yes—I scored much higher than that). But it just goes to illustrate the old point that amateurs built the Ark, and professionals built the Titanic.

But you need to know what you are doing ... because these are perilous times for investors

So you can do this. But it's important you know what you are doing. Because these are perilous times for investors. Things aren't like they used to be.

For example, in the past, markets often seemed to climb steadily for long stretches of time. Like when I was that corporate employee. Investing during those times seemed effortless, brainless really.

The company stock seemed to go up by 15% every year. Me and my fellow employees banked on that fact—we took it for granted — it seemed to happen like clockwork and we assumed we would double our stock value every 5 years based on that fact alone.

I ran into an old chart I had done back then projecting all those numbers. It seems a bit naïve today — to say the least.

And other investors did much the same—they mindlessly bought any old blue chip stocks with a buy and hold attitude. Often this worked.

But not today.

Part 1: Beginnings: Your Choice — The Hard Way Or The Smart Way

So you have a simple choice here—you can do it the hard way like I did, or benefit from my experience and do it the easy way. Now by easy way I don't mean some foolproof method that removes all effort and thought like throwing your money in a mutual fund and hoping for the best. Maybe we'll call it the smart way instead.

Here's the hard way. The markets can climb or fall 400 points in a day. So you buy into an uptrend, thinking it will continue, it drops, you panic and sell at a loss. You bought high and sold low.

You bought high and sold low—oops, that's backwards, isn't it? That's the hard way

Oops, that's backwards, isn't it? You know you are supposed to buy low and sell high. Then you do it again — and again. Loss, loss, loss. It doesn't take too many of these to wipe out your investments.

Or you can see your wins grow by controlling your losses — that's the smart way

And here's the smart way.   You can benefit from my experience learning how to control losses, and over time see your wins outpace your losses.

I learned this one the hard way as I got into the commodities markets years ago.   Commodity markets have often been volatile like this because they are highly leveraged.

For example, when I was trading crude oil, if the price went up a dollar a barrel I made $1000. And if it went down a dollar, I lost $1000. Oops. Note to self: Need to learn how to minimize losses.   It was great real world experience, including the time I almost wiped out one of my commodity accounts before I caught on.

You could go do the same thing, that is, almost wipe out an account, and learn the hard way. I guarantee you this is a learning experience. Or you can take advantage of the stop loss lessons I learned and avoid the pain, taking the smart way.

Or here's another case of the hard way. Markets and stocks can also go into a long downward spiral. And many people hang on, hoping and wishing it will turn around. I call this the hoping, wishing, praying syndrome. And they watch their stocks auger into the ground and can't recover. I learned that one the hard way years ago while trading options on Boeing stock — which I felt sure would turn around. Talk about a plane crash — I rode that one right into the ground.

You can take that plane ride too — another real learning opportunity I assure you — or you can benefit from my experience — taking the smart way —and know when to get out by learning my simple stop loss rule—before you crash land.

You can blindly buy and hold stocks—that's the hard way ... or learn how to find the ones that let you sleep at night—that's the smart way

And you can blindly buy and hold stocks. But those days are over — that leads to the hard way. I said blindly for a reason. Because there are certain stocks you can buy and hold. But you have to know how to find them. I show you this—the smart way — so you can sleep better at night.

But don't try to guess because they aren't necessarily what you think. I know there are stocks out there everyone thinks are great — I mean — it's just common knowledge — but in fact they are not.

That common knowledge can cause you some real financial damage — the hard way. I can think of one stock right now, considered great, that is on the verge of bankruptcy. And just the other day a work associate was telling me proudly how he had invested in it. I mean, he was seriously proud of this investment. It <u>was</u> a great company. <u>Note I said was.</u> Was as in years ago. But not today. He's heading for a crash landing.

You don't want to be doing what he's doing — that's the hard way. Not when you could be learning how to ...
- Find special stocks that truly are buy and hold quality.
- Get better returns on your money
- Review just the bare essentials you need to increase your odds of success.

Now success in the stock market these days may seem an odd turn of phrase to you. After all, I said these are perilous times. And they are.

I said these are perilous times ... but they are not hopeless times

But they are not hopeless times.

Part 1: Beginnings: Your Timing Is Good

We are living at the beginning of an incredible opportunity in the stock market

I'm talking J. Paul Getty-like opportunities

This renaissance in the American oil industry is already creating two millionaires a day ... and it's just beginning

In fact, we are living, at this very moment, at the beginning of an incredible opportunity in the stock market. There is a huge, world-shaking, game-changing event beginning right now as I speak. It is already underway. And most people have not picked up on it yet.

And there is a ton of money to be made from it—in stocks. I'm talking J. Paul Getty-like opportunities, Rockefeller opportunities, like when the railroads started crossing America opportunities — like we can turn back the calendar.

I'm going to ask you a question — and then tell you the answer — which you may find hard to believe. But there is every indication, right now, today, that my incredulous answer is going to come true.

Here's the question.

What country will probably become the biggest oil producer in the world, bigger than Saudi Arabia, within five years?

Here's the answer.

The United States.

Yes—the United States, who to this day continues to spend billions importing oil from the Middle East. This renaissance in the American oil industry is already creating two millionaires a day — and this is just the beginning.

I'm not saying you will become a millionaire, but do you sense an investment opportunity here? If you knew how to find these stocks, and manage them the right way, would you not have more confidence, a more in control feeling, sleep better at night and have more hope for the future?.

This world shaking opportunity is right in front of you. And this book is in your hands. So you have a choice. You can spend the twenty-one years I did, do all my research, and make all of my mistakes I learned from. That's the hard way.

Or you can take the smart way and learn what we'll cover and how. Why not find out what it's all about?

Part 1: Beginnings: What We'll Cover And How

So here's what we're going to do, and how.

We introduce this subject to you in terms you already understand

First, we'll introduce the subject areas to you in terms you already know and understand. That's a breakthrough idea. Let me show you with a quick example.

You know what an auction is, right? Well, did you know that the New York Stock Exchange – where you will buy many of your stocks -- is just a big auction?

See, you already have a clue about stock exchanges. Because we introduced the idea with something you already understand. An auction.

Second, we outline a basic, step by step plan on how you get set up, choose your stocks and protect your investment. And we keep it simple and stick to buying and selling stocks and stock based products. Nothing else.

Here's how we're going to do that.

There's no point in doing something unless we understand the purpose

So why do we want to invest anyway? The answers may surprise you

First we'll consider why we should invest. I think you'll agree there's no point in doing something unless we understand the purpose. So I'll give you my perspectives on why investing is important. A couple of them may surprise you – like the concepts of "sitting at the other side of the table," and "money machines."

Next we cover a few basics – and I mean a few. There are about ten of them. Like "what is a share of stock," and "what is the New York Stock Exchange." And most important, that with your first stock purchase you become a business owner. Congratulations.

Then we'll ask you to think on what are your goals …. We'll talk about a few of these but we keep it simple. Your goals will have to do with creating wealth, or income, or both.

We will discuss some of the types of investments out there. We're going to keep that simple too. They will be primarily stocks and stock-like investments, but we'll cover a few more – just for your information.

Then it's time to get started. Time to take some action. So we discuss how you need a stock trading account and a discount broker, how to choose a broker, the one I use, what your account will look like and how to set it up.

Now that we're set up, what stocks do we buy? Here I share with you how I pick the stocks I invest in. I'll give you a hint. I let someone else do the research for me -- even though I was a Financial Consultant, and licensed with the New York Stock Exchange as a broker. I've used these researchers for over ten years. I tell you who they are and why I use them.

Okay, so we read our research and found a stock with a great story. Now how do we buy that stock? You'll learn how to place your order.

But that's just technique.

One of my favorite buying techniques involves what I call the Warren Buffett mindset

We also outline the smart way to buy. It has to do with your mindset. I call it the Warren Buffett mindset. And with the research you will have at hand, it will be easier to maintain this mindset.

Of course, once we've made an investment, we don't want to lose the money. So I tell you two specific techniques I use to minimize the losses and maximize the gains. You must do both of these to succeed.   But they are not complicated.

And finally, now that you're set up and own some stocks, what do you do now? What do you do, day to day. We wrap up with that one.   And you're on your way.

You can take this course at your own pace and start investing with a little money or a lot. Because we're going to take this one small step at a time.

Remember, the greatest investors in the world started where you are today. Even Warren Buffett, one of the wealthiest, most successful investors in the world, started where you are right now.

So relax and set your frustrations aside. Because with your effort and our method – you can do this!

So let's get started with the most important question? Why

do we want to invest, anyway? Some of the answers may surprise you.

PART 2: Why Invest In Stocks?

So You Can Sit At The Other Side Of The Table

Stocks Are The Easiest Way To Be A Business Owner

Am I Really A Business Owner?

You Can Think of Stocks as Money Machines

Isn't Stock Investing Just Gambling With Your Money?

Stocks Can Help You Achieve Your Goals

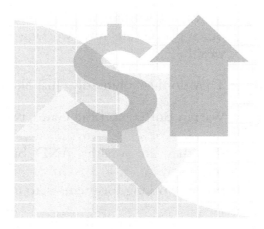

So You Can Sit At The Other Side Of The Table

People spend more time planning their next vacation than their financial future

Stock investing seats you at the other side of the table

It's said that people spend more time planning their next vacation than planning for their investments and financial future.

When I was a financial consultant and licensed stockbroker, I often found this to be the case. And hey, I get that. A vacation is fun and in the near future. So it's easy to visualize. And fun to think about.

Still, many people have this vague, uneasy feeling that they should know a bit more about investments — and that they should be doing something about them — and soon.

So why bother with investing?

Because stock investing seats you at the other side of the table. You become a business owner instead of an employee.

Instead of working for someone else, to increase their wealth, other people are now working for you ... to increase your wealth.

They do this voluntarily. Just like you go to work, voluntarily.

Warren Buffett and Bill Gates, two of the wealthiest people in the world, are business owners. It's not a coincidence that they are wealthy AND business owners. As business owners, they sit at the other side of the table. They have people working for them — to increase their wealth.

And investing in stock is the easiest way to become a business owner.

It's the easiest way to sit at the other side of the table.

So which side of the table do you want to sit on? The worker side, or the business owner side with Warren Buffett and Bill Gates. I'm thinking the business owner side.

So remember, you are buying stock to become a business

owner, so other people work for you voluntarily to increase your wealth.

You are buying stocks to sit at the other side of the table.

Stocks Are The Easiest Way To Be A Business Owner

Many of the wealthiest people have done so by owning businesses

We just discussed how many of the wealthiest people in the world have become so by owning businesses.

And that two of the wealthiest people in the world are Bill Gates and Warren Buffett. They both own businesses. And this is no coincidence.

Stock investing is really much the same as owning a business.

We also said that stock investing is the easiest way to own a business. So consider for a moment what it would take to start and run a business. We'll contrast that to an investment in a business.

In order to own a business, you may need to have a store. This will involve a real estate purchase or lease and the complications and obligations that go along with it. You'll need to make sure the store is opened on time and closed at the end of the day. The store will need to be kept clean and maintained.

But when you buy stock to invest in a business other people take care of all of that for you.

You will certainly need to attract customers. This is actually the most important aspect of owning a successful business. Otherwise, you will be going out of business.

But when you invest in a business, marketing and sales people take care of that for you.

And you will need to purchase a lot of inventory to start your business. Otherwise, you have nothing to sell to your customers – that is to say, if you can attract them in the first place.

But when you buy stock to invest in a business, that's taken care of already.

I'm getting a headache just thinking about all of this – and there are many more things I haven't even mentioned.

PART 2: Why Invest In Stocks?

For instance, four out of five new businesses fail. That's not very good odds if you ask me.

What if that happens to you and your business? How do you get out of all these obligations, liquidate all that inventory, and everything else you need to do to shut it down? How long is that going to take?

When you own a business this can take weeks, months, even years. To illustrate this point, it's like the difference between trying to sell your house or selling a real estate stock that you own.

Selling your house can take weeks, months or years (how's that working out for you these days?). Selling a real estate stock can be done in seconds. Some difference, yes?

To be a successful stock investor, you need the same mindset as a business owner

Okay, so enough said about owning a business for now. We're here to take the easier route – to buy stocks to invest in a business.

But I want you to remember one thing. You are now going into business when you invest. It's easier than actually starting your business.

But you need the same mindset as a business owner.

Am I Really A Business Owner?

Are you REALLY a business owner when you own stocks? Yes, in virtually everyway you are a business owner. As an owner of a share of stock you are really a LEGAL business owner.

Think of one of your favorite companies and products. Like Coach handbags, or McDonalds, or Pizza Hut. If you own a share of their stock, you are a legal business owner.

If you own a share of stock, the people in that company work for you

You will own a share of their profits. And you may be asked to vote for or against a pay raise for their top executives — that sounds like a business owner to me.

You will be sent an annual report telling you how well your business did that year. The people who go to work every day in those companies work for you.

The Chief Executive Officer works for you. The Chairman of the Board and the Board Members are working for your interest.

They all go to work every day to increase your wealth. Everybody works for you.

As an owner of stocks in a company, you are a business owner.

Here's the really great thing about all of that. You don't have to do anything. That has a nice sound to it, doesn't it?

You Can Think Of Stocks As Money Machines

Wouldn't it be nice if you could go to Walmart and buy a money machine?

Here's another way I like to think about stocks. I like to think I am buying money machines.

Wouldn't it be nice if you could go down to Wal-Mart and pay $49.95 for a money machine. And you could buy as many of them as you wanted. Maybe every week you bought another one. That's fifty-two money machines in a year.

You just set the little money machines in the closet and forget about them. And every three months they would dump $.50 on the floor. That's a little over four cents a week per machine.

So the first week you'd have 4 cents, the next week you buy another so you have two machines so you would get 8 cents that week, the next week three machines so you'd get 12 cents, on and on for fifty-two weeks. At the end of the first year you'd have over 5700 pennies just laying all over the floor. What a mess. But that's a $57 mess.

Now you could spend that $57. Or here's a thought. You take most of that $57 and buy one more money machine. Why not, it's paid for. The other money machines bought it for you.

Now you have 53 money machines sitting in the closet. But it gets better. Because maybe next year all of your money machines start dumping out a little more money than they did last year — let's say $.55 at a time instead of $.50.

At the end of the second year you'd have 11236 pennies laying all over the floor. That's over $112. Now you can buy two more money machines. And the machines keep on increasing how many pennies each one puts out by a little bit each year.

And we haven't even talked about the fact that the price of the money machines goes up, so the ones you own are worth more now. Maybe they are all worth $55 instead of the $49.95 you paid for them.

PART 2: Why Invest In Stocks?

That's how many stocks work. Interestingly, a share of Wal-Mart stock would cost about as much as our example and dump that much money on your closet floor.

So let's think about this for a minute. You can go out and spend your money on a new car, which is worth less as soon as you drive it off the dealers lot. And it costs you money to drive it.

Or you can go buy a nice dinner at a restaurant, which is gone as soon as you eat it.

Or you can buy money machines.

Nothing against new cars and nice dinners, I like them both. I'm just saying they lose value over time – rather quickly.

But your money machines dump out a little bit of money every three months, year after year and they become worth more over time.

Talk About A Money Machine – This One Dumped Out $768 Every Three Months

I invested in Mark West Energy, a natural gas pipeline company, in 2008 when the market was down. I was fortunate enough to have $10,000 to invest.

They paid me $768 every three months in dividends. So I was getting 20% on my investment just in dividends. Plus, my investment grew to $28,000 in 18 months.

Talk about a money machine!

Does that get your attention. Does this seem like a good reason to invest? Not all stocks will do this well. But it does happen.

By the way, I got the research and investment idea for this stock from one of the financial newsletters I recommend in a later chapter.

And I'm still getting the 20% dividend.

Isn't Stock Investing Just Gambling With Your Money?

I hear this question quite often. My first answer is no, investing is not necessarily the same as gambling.

However, the way most people invest, for all intents and purposes, is gambling. That's why you hear of them giving up because they lose money all the time.

Let's think about true gambling for a moment. When you are flipping a coin and betting on the result – that is gambling.

Why?

When gambling by flipping a coin, there is no amount of research you can do to discover if the next flip is more likely to be heads (or tails)

Because there is no amount of research you can do to discover if this flip is more likely to be heads (or tails). And there is no action you can take in advance that will influence the outcome. The odds are always 50-50 for every coin flip.

Now consider a stock investment. There is all kinds of research you can do in advance that can increase your odds of making a good stock pick.

You can investigate things like the following for example …
- Has there been a lot of insider buying recently?
- Does the company have solid finances or is it heavily in debt?
- Has it's sales and profits been increasing consistently over time?
- Is the management experienced in the industry with a long track record of success?
- Has the company paid a dividend consistently for years and increased it's dividend every year?

And there are many other aspects of the business concerning it's chances for success. There are many clues here, don't you think?

Take one, for example — insider buying. Insiders sell and buy shares of their company all of the time. There are many reasons why insiders might sell, i.e. they think the stock might go down, or they have a child's college tuition coming due or

PART 2: Why Invest In Stocks?

they just need the cash.

But there's only one reason why insiders buy stock in their company. They see prospects are good and the stock may be going up in the future. So if you see a high level executive in a company suddenly buy 100,000 shares of the company's stock, that's telling you something.

Of course, even with many clues, there are no guarantees in life and especially in the stock market, but *doing this kind of research in advance greatly increases your odds of a good outcome over time.*

You can even buy this research for a very reasonable price if you don't want to do it yourself (which is what I do – I told you we were going to do this the easy way).

But you can't do anything like this before you bet on heads or tails of a coin flip. And there is no research you can buy either. The odds are always 50-50.

The way the average investor chooses stocks probably is like gambling ...

Now consider how the average investor chooses stocks. They probably don't do any research at all. So they effectively throw away every advantage investing in stocks has over pure gambling. So in their case, it is essentially gambling. And they get the same unfortunate result.

... because they throw away every advantage investing in stocks has over pure gambling

But if you follow the research and other simple steps outlined in this book, you will greatly increase your odds of success with your investments. But you have to do them all.

And if you do, you will not be gambling. You will be investing. There's a big difference.

Get A Clue From Insider Buying

Many forms of insider buying are completely legal and you can improve your odds by knowing when it's happening.

Insider buying is a matter of public record and is very easy to research. One place you can look is in Yahoo Finance. Just go to www.Yahoo.com, click the Finance option, pick the stock you are interested in and click the insider buying tab.

You'll see some VERY interesting information.

Stocks Can Help You Achieve Your Goals

This is perhaps the most important reason to invest in stocks. They can help you achieve your goals. So you should take some time and consider what your goals are before you get started. This will guide the types of investments you make in the future.

When I was a stockbroker we were always told to "know your customer." Since you are taking charge of your financial life, and now your own customer, it pays to, as Plato said, "know thyself."

That said, I'm not going to go into any big goal setting dialogue here. There is plenty of good material written about that. But here are some thoughts to consider.

Not enough people are saving for retirement ... I read recently that the Baby Boomers may be the first generation not able to retire

Saving for Retirement. This is one of the main reasons people invest. They set aside a percent of their income and invest it so it will provide them income when they retire. Put another way, they work for their money for many years so their money can work for them later in life.

Not enough people are doing this in sufficient amounts. I read recently that the baby boomers may be the first generation that cannot retire. So I would encourage you to take a good look at this goal.

Generating Retirement Income Today. You really should consult with a retirement counselor on this, but here are some thoughts.

Your focus is very much on protecting your retirement nest egg and generating income to live off of. So you will be more interested in dividend paying stocks and fixed income investments like bonds.

It used to be that people in this category would have more bonds in their accounts, but with the historic low interest rates, this doesn't work as well today. And there are some solid world dominating stocks that are actually paying greater dividends today than the more conservative bond investments. And there are analysts that feel some of these stocks carry no greater risk.

So many investment newsletters advise a higher percentage of solid, dividend paying stocks to make up for the low interest rates than was recommended in the past.

Only you can decide this. The best indicator will be how well you sleep at night with the investment mix you pick. But stocks will be part of most people's portfolio to some extent to help keep up with inflation.

Saving For College. You may be investing and saving to fund college tuition for your children. Given the high cost of tuition these days, stocks and other investments can help you achieve this goal.

Have Your Money Work For You. This is a great reason to invest. After all, you work hard for your money, why not make it work for you as well.

Investing For The Thrill Of It. Okay, now we're starting to get close to the gambler mentality.

While there definitely can be a thrill to investing (sometimes too much of a thrill), you need to be careful with this one or you will just lose all of your money.

If you must, just set aside 5% of your investment funds for high flying, risky stocks

A good suggestion I've seen some financial advisors make is to use 5% of your investments for the more high flying risky stocks. This way you get it out of your system. And you may actually hit the jackpot, or more likely, if you don't, you have only lost 5% of your account.

Learning About The Stock Market. This is a pretty good goal to my way of thinking. Because things can get pretty emotional when you have money on the table as opposed to just reading and thinking about investments in theory.

The more you know before you put money on the table, the more likely you are to invest, buy and sell rationally. But at some point you have to act and make an investment. So don't use this as an excuse for "analysis paralysis."

Any other personal investment goals and reasons you may

PART 2: Why Invest In Stocks?

have.

The point of this chapter is to encourage you to think about what you are trying to accomplish with your investments. But I wouldn't over think it. Just consider all the reasons and then get started.

So lets do just that. Let's get started by covering a few basics, like what is the New York Stock Exchange anyway.

$$\begin{array}{r} \$250{,}000 \\ X\ .04 \\ \hline \$10{,}000 \end{array}$$

EXTRA CREDIT: Retirement Rule Of Thumb

Here is a rough rule of thumb for how much you will need. For every $10,000 in income per year you will need in retirement, you may need $250,000 in investment savings.

That amount takes into consideration future inflation and spends none of your $250,000.

Here is the way that thinking goes.

It assumes you will make 8% on average on your investments. It assumes inflation will average 4% of that – so you won't spend that – it helps you keep even with inflation.

And it assumes you will use the other 4% of investment income to live on. So 4% of $250,000 is $10,000 a year to live on.

Note that this is just a rough guide. Also note you spend none of your $250,000 in this example. Most people will begin to draw this down as they get later into retirement.

Also note that *I STRONGLY ADVISE that you see a qualified retirement counselor or financial consultant to plan all of this out* for your specific situation and assets. This book cannot address your unique, overall financial situation.

PART 3: Understanding The Basics

Stocks and The Stock Market

What Is A Share Of Stock

What Is The New York Stock Exchange (NYSE)

What Is The NASDAQ and OTC

How Do I Know Which Exchange To Use?

What Is A Stock Symbol?

What Are Bulls And Bears?

What Does Long And Short Mean?

What Is My Share Of Stock Worth?

Those Pesky Percents

What Is A Share Of Stock?

When you invest in stocks, you actually buy shares of stock. So what is a share of stock anyway?

Let's think about a pizza pie. And lets say you and your friends all chip in and buy a pie together. So you will all **share** slices of the pizza pie. I just said the word "**share**," didn't I.

So you cut the pie into slices. And you **share** the slices with your friends. They each got their **shares** of slices and you get your **share**.

Now let's say you and your friends want to buy a business together. Maybe a nice wine shop to go with the pizza. So you will all **share** the business.

You cut (divide) the ownership of the business into slices (**shares**). And you share the ownership (slices, **shares**) with your friends. They each get their **share** and you get your **share**.

That's all a share of stock is. It's your slice (share) of the business. It's your share of the ownership. It's your share of the profits. It's your share.

Corporations slice their ownership into millions of shares

Corporations slice their ownership up into shares also. Anyone can buy a share. Or you can buy more than one share.

Just like our pizza example — let's say it cost you $10 and you cut it into 10 slices. That's $1.00 a slice. If you were really hungry, you could have chipped in $2.00 so you would get two slices. So you bought two shares.

Of course corporations are a lot bigger than a $10 pizza pie. So they cut the ownership into millions of shares.

You can buy more than one share. You can buy 12 shares, or 100 shares, or a 1000 shares. You can buy as many shares as you want and can afford.

But it is exactly the same idea as your 10 shares of pizza pie. You are buying your slice(s) of the corporate pie. You are

PART 3: Understanding The Basics

buying your share(s).

EXTRA CREDIT: Pizza Hut is one of the largest pizza companies in the world. They are owned by YUM Brands Corporation.

Do you know how many slices (shares) they have divided their corporation into? (I don't really expect you to know this).

Answer: 466,000,000 shares. Each share costs about $50. If you bought all of the shares it would cost over 23 billion dollars ($23,000,000,000) to buy the whole corporation.

Isn't it nice they slice the company up into many little shares

What Is The New York Stock Exchange?

The New York Stock Exchange is just an auction. You know, like an auction where there's a guy talking real fast to a bunch of buyers to sell Grandma Mable's rocking chair and other furniture so she can move to Florida to be near her grandkids.

And different people keep bidding a higher and higher price until someone discovers they bid the highest price and now they own the rocking chair.

That's all the New York Stock Exchange (NYSE) is, really. An auction.

The New York Stock Exchange (NYSE) is just a big auction

But instead of selling rocking chairs, they sell shares of stock in different companies. And whoever bids the highest price just bought the stock.

Also, the NYSE is an auction on steroids. Because instead of one auctioneer selling one thing at a time to a bunch of people, it's a bunch of people selling and buying stocks from each other all at once.

They are out in the open on the floor of the NYSE crying out buy and sell orders to each other all at once and making all kinds of noise.

This is why it is called the "open outcry" system. Really. And it is so noisy many of them use hand signals as well.

It is one gigantic, noisy bunch of auctions all happening at once on the floor of the exchange as they trade stocks with each other. So you won't be surprised when I tell you they are called "floor traders."

Actually, I should say they WERE called floor traders. Because today this isn't done so much. Instead, the traders are buying and selling and holding all their simultaneous auctions with each other on their computers.

But it's still the same thing — just not as noisy. It's an auction. Kind of like E-Bay. But much faster.

So when you buy or sell a stock, one of these traders gets your order and jumps into the auction to buy or sell it for

PART 3: Understanding The Basics

you. And you get the best price that another person is willing to pay.

Just like an auction, your shares of stock don't have a fixed price. They are only worth what someone will pay at the big auction. But we will get into that more later.

For now, all you need to remember is that the New York Stock Exchange is just a big auction. And they sell shares of stock at their auction.

EXTRA CREDIT: When the Dutch had settled in New York around the year 1640 there was a big earthen wall on the northern end of their settlement, presumably to keep out Indians and other encroachers (although the Indians may have had a different point of view on who exactly were the encroachers). A street ran along this wall and it became known as Wall Street.

Later, in the 1700's, at the foot of Wall Street, traders and speculators would gather under an old buttonwood tree to trade stocks and securities. And in 1792 they formalized their association with the Buttonwood Agreement which was the origin of the New York Stock Exchange. The New York Stock Exchange is still located on Wall Street today. It's street and mailing address is …

NYSE Group, Inc.
11 Wall Street
New York, NY 10005

What Are The NASDAQ and OTC?

Different auctions sell different kinds of merchandise ... just like different stock exchanges sell different kinds of company's stocks

There are different kinds of auctions that sell different kinds of things.

For example, some auctions sell expensive things like fine art. Other auctions sell cheaper things, like Grandma Mable's rocking chair (not saying anything against Grandma Mable here). And some auctions sell technical things like computers, lets say.

There are big expensive companies sold on the NYSE

We talked about the New York Stock Exchange (NYSE). It's a big auction that sells shares of stock in the big, expensive companies. It's kind of like the expensive, fine art auction.

You would never find Grandma Mable's rocking chair at a fine art auction. So there's another exchange (auction) that sells smaller, cheaper companies.

Smaller, cheaper companies are sold on the OTC

It's called **the Over The Counter Market (OTC)**. It's more like the lower priced rocking chair / furniture auction. Not knocking the companies that are sold here. They are just much smaller companies, many of which are just getting started. Some of these startup companies offer incredible profit opportunities if you have good research and pick the right one.

And then there's an auction that sells shares of stock in technology companies — like Microsoft. It's kind of like our computer auction. It's called **the NASDAQ, which stands for National Association of Securities Dealers Automated Quotations.** Say that fast three times. Or do what everyone else does and just say Naz' Dack.

And technology companies are sold on the NASDAQ

Anyhow, that's all you need to know.

Your stocks are bought and sold in different exchanges (auctions). Which means you will buy and sell your stocks on different exchanges, depending on what type of stock it is.

If you are concerned about knowing which exchange to use, don't worry; just read on. You'll like the answer in the next chapter.

PART 3: Understanding The Basics

EXTRA CREDIT: The Over The Counter (OTC) cheaper stocks are sometimes referred to as Pink Sheets. That's because years ago they would print their stocks on pink paper and their bonds on yellow paper.

This was probably done to keep their stocks and bonds from getting mixed up, wouldn't you say? Good idea.

EXTRA EXTRA CREDIT: The Over The Counter (OTC) Market isn't technically really an exchange like The New York Stock Exchange.

But for you and me it really doesn't matter. It works for us just like any other exchange.

I just told you this one so you can impress someone or win a bet at a party. If they press you about why it is different, just quickly offer to go freshen their drink.

How Do I Know Which Exchange To Use?

We just discussed how different types of companies stocks are sold on different exchanges. So when you want to buy a stock, how do you know which exchange to use?

You're going to like this answer.

You don't need to worry about it.

Because when you go to buy a stock, it will automatically go to the right exchange. For example, if you place an order to buy Microsoft shares, it will automatically go to the NASDAQ exchange.

If you place an order to buy Sprint stock, it will automatically go to the New York Stock Exchange (NYSE).

That's where these different stocks are traded. Isn't that easy?

Wouldn't it be nice if everything was like that (like understanding your phone or medical insurance bill)?

What Is A Stock Symbol?

Often you will see stocks referred to as a short series of letters – like MSFT, or S or GOOG. This is called a stock symbol and it's really pretty simple.

Each stock has a short, unique abbreviation assigned to it. No other stock has that abbreviation. For example, the abbreviation for Microsoft is MSFT. No other stock can use the abbreviation MSFT.

So when you see MSFT, that ALWAYS means people are talking about shares of Microsoft stock. Or when you see S, that is ALWAYS Sprint. And when you see GOOG, that is Google.

Stock symbols are just a short abbreviation of the stock so people don't have to key in the entire name. Imagine if you worked in the financial industry and had to write out the full company name every time during the day.

So that's all a stock symbol is really – just a unique abbreviation for a stock. It's that simple.

EXTRA CREDIT: The stock symbol is sometimes called a ticker symbol. This is because years before computers were used, they used a small machine called a ticker tape to print the symbols and prices on a paper tape during the day.

The little machine was really just a sophisticated telegraph machine that printed on the tape.

When it was printing the stock symbols and latest prices, it made a ticking noise – hence the name ***ticker symbol.***

EXTRA EXTRA CREDIT: The little ticker machines were very slow – and they printed slow too.

So this was another reason stock symbols (abbreviations) were created. So they could keep up with the rapid trading in the market during the day.

And it also saved paper tape. Good idea.

The little machines made a ticking sound as they printed the stock symbols and prices ... hence the name ticker symbol

Tick, tick...

What Are Bulls And Bears?

Bull markets go up and are good ...

... and bear markets go down and are bad ...

... well, kinda, sorta true more or less. Bear markets are often necessary corrections in the market and offer you the opportunity to buy great stocks on sale

You may hear people talk about bull markets and bear markets. So what are these bulls and bears they are talking about?

Well, everyone knows what a bull is. It's a very aggressive animal. It charges forward. So when the stock market is going up, it's charging forward aggressively, confidently — like a bull.

Most people like that because it means their stocks are going up in value, charging forward, aggressively. They are charging forward toward their financial goals and dreams.

So bull markets are good. Everybody likes them.

How about the bears?

Well, bears are big scary animals that terrify people. Just like when the stock market is going down. The value of people's shares is going down, and they get scared.

They fear all their financial hopes and dreams are going to run away, and they start to panic — like if a bear was chasing them.

So bear markets are bad. Nobody likes them much.

Anyhow, that's the simple answer. However, all bear markets are not necessarily bad, as long as they don't get out of hand. These are called corrections and are necessary because sometimes the prices of stocks get too high in relation to the values of the companies.

So then some people start selling their stocks at these high prices to take profits. And that usually brings the stock price back down in line to the true value of the company.

So you can do a couple of things with bear markets. You can protect yourself from them — which we cover later. Or you can look at most of them as a way to buy great stocks on sale.

And that's a good thing.

PART 3: Understanding The Basics

EXTRA CREDIT: There is a big statue of a large animal near Wall Street in New York. Can you guess what it is?

Answer: It's a bull. Everybody likes bull markets.

EXTRA EXTRA CREDIT: Believe it or not, there are some people that like bear markets. There's always that ten percent that just don't get the word, yes? Or maybe they are onto something.

Remember, a bear market is when the market goes down as stocks lose some of their value. Some people that like bear markets have done something called short selling. They actually make money when stocks go down. What's not to like about that?

Short selling is a more advanced technique we discuss in the Long and Short chapter. But don't worry about that. We won't be shorting any stocks at this level of investing. You don't ever have to short stocks or understand the concept if you don't want to.

You can do just fine being happy when the market goes up. And it's normal to worry when the market goes down. So the normal attitude is to like bull markets and not like bear markets.

What Does Long And Short Mean?

"Long" and "Short" are terms you will hear sometimes and you will also see them in your stock account, so it's good that you know what they mean.

Long simply means you are trading a stock that you own

Fortunately, the term "Long" is what you will be involved in and is the easiest to understand. **Long simply means you are trading a stock that you own.** It's that simple. So when you are "Long" a stock, it means you own it.

When you are "Long" a stock, that means you have bought the stock because you believe the price will go higher. You are doing this in hopes that you can sell it at the higher price in the future and keep the difference as a profit.

Here are two sentences that mean EXACTLY the same thing.
1) *I OWN ten shares of Microsoft stock.*
2) *I am LONG ten shares of Microsoft stock.*

In other words, you are trying to "buy low" and "sell high."

Most investors do this. In fact, this is probably the only way you have ever thought about investing in stocks. That's fine because this is the only way recommended in this book at this trading level.

Short means you are trading a stock you DON"T OWN. You borrowed it

Short means you are trading a stock you don't own. You borrowed it. You didn't buy it (like if you were long). Since you won't be shorting stocks we will leave the explanation at that.

However, if you are curious, just read the extra credit section below. We get into shorting stocks in the next book in our training series called ***Beyond Stock Investing For Beginners.***

Caution: **DO NOT SHORT STOCKS** until you understand the concept completely. **Shorting stocks can put you in a position of UNLIMITED LIABILITY. By that I mean you can potentially lose the value of you investment, your house, your car, your anything of value.**

EXTRA CREDIT: Believe it or not, it is also possible to make money when stocks go down. This is done by being "Short" a stock.

For those that are curious about how you make money when

PART 3: Understanding The Basics

a stock goes down, read on.

When you are "Short" a stock, that means you have **borrowed** the stock and sold it — which immediately puts cash in your account. Nice.

You did this because you believe the price will go down. To make money, you hope you can buy the stock at a lower price in the future, give those borrowed shares back, and keep the difference as a profit.

In other words, you are trying to "sell high" and then "buy low." Notice in both cases, whether you are long or short, you are trying to buy LOW and sell HIGH and keep the difference as profit. It's just which you do first. Do you buy first or sell first.

Here's a different kind of example of a short. Lets say your neighbor has a 2010 Ford worth $20,000 that he doesn't use. You both agree that you can borrow his Ford for six months. He doesn't care if he gets his original Ford back in six months – he just wants the same kind of 2010 Ford returned to him.

Congratulations — you just shorted a 2010 Ford

You are pretty sure the price of 2010 Fords is going to go down to $15,000 in six months. So you borrow his Ford and immediately sell it for $20,000. Sure enough, six months later you are able to buy the same kind of 2010 Ford for $15,000. So you buy it.

You give him back the Ford you just bought for $15,000. Your neighbor is happy. He now has a 2010 Ford again. And you are happy. You get to keep the $5000 difference in price.

PART 3: Understanding The Basics

What Is My Share Of Stock Worth?

Remember, your share of stock is bought and sold at an auction. So it's only worth whatever the highest bidder is willing to pay for it when you sell it.

Or if you are buying, a stock is worth the lowest amount the seller is willing to sell it for.

So you are always in competition with the other buyers and sellers. Even if you are not selling your stocks, their value changes all through the day — because it's an all day auction every day.

So WHEN you buy and sell a stock is important. We'll get into that later.

Just remember that your shares of stock are worth more or less every minute of every day. They don't have a fixed price.

Just like an auction.

The value of your shares can go up or down every minute of every day

Those Pesky Percents

Cent is a Latin word that means hundred. There are 100 cents in a dollar. Coincidence?

You will be seeing percents in your investing. And let's face it -- some people have problems with percents.

Fortunately you won't have to know too much about them using the Stock Market For Beginners way to invest. Just the basics. But just in case you have a bit of a problem with percents, here's a simple way to understand them – and I bet you get this.

Just think of dollars and cents. Everyone knows there are 100 cents in a dollar. All the word cent means is one hundred (it's a Latin word, actually). So **"per cent"** just means "per **hundred.**" That's all it means. Get it?

So if someone says they made 8 percent, that means they made 8 cents per (for) every 100 cents they invested. If they invested 100 cents, now they have 8 more cents. So now they have 108 cents (or $1.08).

And if they say they made 100 percent, now they have 100 cents more for every 100 cents (a dollar) they invested. So now they have 200 cents (or $2.00).

Here are two sentences that mean EXACTLY the same thing.

1) *There are 5 apples PER HUNDRED in that big bag of mixed fruit*

2) *There are 5 PER CENT apples in that big bag of mixed fruit*

So whatever the percent is, just pretend it's cents and add it to a dollar (which has 100 cents). That's how many cents you have after the investment.

Pretty simple isn't it?

Now, people usually invest more than one dollar. So lets say you invested $1000. And let's say you made 8 percent.

That means you made 8 cents for every dollar. Since you invested a thousand dollars, you made 8000 cents (1000 times the 8 cents). That's 8000 cents, or $80.

So now you have your original $1000 plus the $80 for a total of $1080.

Or if you want to shortcut this and use a formula, it is …

How much you invested X the percent / 100.
How much you invested is $1000. The percent is 8. So you

PART 3: Understanding The Basics

can enter **1000 X 8 / 100 =** into your calculator just like that. This will give you the correct answer of $80.

Or you can use the percent key on a calculator, in which case you would enter **8 + 1000 % =** which will give you the correct answer of $80.

Here are some illustrative thoughts on some sample percents and investment expectations. Note that some years you may lose money.

- **You invested a $1000 and made 8% in a year.** So at the end of the year you have $1080. *That is the average return stocks have yielded over the past 90 years +-.* That beats the heck out of 1% or less interest at a bank.

- **You invested $1000 and made 20% in a year.** So at the end of the year you had $1200. *That is an outstanding return on your investment.* At that rate you will double your investment in under four years.

- **You invested $1000 and made 100% in a year.** So at the end of the year you had $2000. *That is a screaming great return on your investment. You should be writing this book, not me.* Actually I have done this a few times, but it does not happen for every investment, nor should you expect it. Many of the stock newsletters I recommend bag a few of these most years. That's why I use them.

That's all you need to know. Your investment statements and online screens will show the percents and dollars for you. Now you know how they do it and what it means.

EXTRA CREDIT: Why does the first formula divide by 100?
1000 X 8 / 100 =

Answer: Because you are doing things *per hundred*, or *per cent*. Cent means hundred.

PART 4: Different Types Of Investments

Are You Loaning Or Owning?

Cash

Money Market

Stock Based Investments

Other Types Of Investments

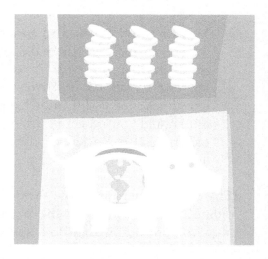

Are You Loaning Or Owning?

Investments break down into two categories— you are either LOANING or OWNING

I break investments down into two categories. **You are either loaning or owning.** Below are a number of examples to illustrate this point. But I bet you get the picture in the first two.

If you buy a CD at the bank you are loaning them your money. They pay you interest for the use of it. The interest is how you make money.

If you buy a stock you are OWNING

If you buy a stock, you are owning. You are now an owner of the business. It may pay you dividends from the profits of the business and you are betting the company (and it's stock) will become more valuable. This is how you make money.

If you buy a bond you are LOANING

If you buy a corporate bond, you are loaning. You are loaning money to a corporation. They will pay you interest for the use of it. This is how you make money.

If you buy a fine art oil painting, you are owning. You are betting that the painting will appreciate in value. This is how you make money.

Okay, so you get the picture. By and large, investments are either loaning or owning.

So what is the overall tradeoff? Well, loaning (bonds, etc.) is considered safer but you make less money. Owning (stocks) is considered more risky, but offers the chance of a higher return.

Since this is a book on stock investing, we will only cover how to buy and sell stocks (and stock-like investments). *So we will be owning.* However, that is not to say that bonds and other "loaning" investments should not be part of your portfolio.

PART 4: Different Types Of Investments

We will stay focused on buying stocks (OWNING) and master that important area of investment

But for most people, stocks will be a significant part of their investment portfolio. So if you master this material, you could do well for yourself in that important area of your investments

So that's it. We will be focusing on owning. That is to say we will focus on buying stocks in this book. To try to do more could be overwhelming. So we'll stay focused and master this material.

There are only two simple exceptions to this—which you will understand immediately. These are covered in the next chapter.

EXTRA CREDIT: Generally, the younger you are, the more stocks (owning) and less bonds / CD's / Treasuries (loaning) you will have, although those guidelines have shifted more toward stocks recently. The shift has been brought on by the low interest rates, forcing people more toward stocks where they can get a better return.

EXTRA EXTRA CREDIT: MORE LOANING AND OWNING
For those interested, here are some more loaning or owning examples. See how just about every investment you can imagine breaks down into one of these categories.

If you buy a 10 year U. S. Treasury note, you are loaning. You are loaning the United States federal government money. They will pay you interest for the use of it. This is how you make money.

If you buy a commodities contract of 1000 barrels of crude oil, you are owning. You are betting the price of oil will go up before the contract comes due for delivery. This is how you are making money.

If your friend asks you for a $10,000 loan to start a business, you are loaning. The 6% interest he says he'll pay you is how you will make money.

If your friend asks you to invest $10,000 in his new business as a 50-50 partner, you are owning. You are betting the business will be profitable, and you will share in the profits. This is how you will make money.

If you invest in a bond mutual fund, you are loaning. The fund is buying a mix of bonds in corporations and /or U. S. Treasuries, which will pay it interest, which it distributes to you. This is how you make money.

If you buy pure silver coins, you are OWNING

If you go out and buy 10 one ounce pure silver Canadian Maple Leaf coins, you are owning. You are betting the price of silver will go up in the future. This is how you will make your money.

If you invest in a stock mutual fund, you are owning. The mutual fund is investing in shares of corporations, which will pay dividends out of profits, and hopefully the company and its shares will go up in value, and this will be distributed to you. This is how you make your money.

If you buy a balanced mutual fund, you are LOANING and OWNING

If you invest in a balanced mutual fund, you are loaning AND owning. The mutual fund will invest in some bonds and / or U. S. Treasuries (loaning) which will pay interest. It will also buy shares in stocks (owning) which will pay dividends and hopefully increase in value. The interest, dividends and increased share value will be distributed to you. This is how you make your money.

PART 4: Different Types Of Investments

Cash

Cash in itself is a poor investment over the long term

Cash in itself is a poor investment over the long term. It loses value every year due to inflation – on average about three percent.

Many investors mistakenly believe they should be fully invested and keep little cash in their account

Many investors keep little or no cash in their account because they feel they should be fully invested. Successful investors do not do this. They always hold some cash in reserve so they can take advantage of buying good stocks at deep discounts during market downturns. Nothing increases your odds of success better than buying good stocks on sale.

Professionals usually keep some cash in their accounts to take advantage of bargain stock prices when there is a market downturn

Opinions vary widely on how much of your investment portfolio should be kept in cash. A good rule of thumb is 10% to 20% under normal circumstances. But depending on market conditions, I have seen financial professionals recommend as much as 40% to 50% and a few heading for the hills at 100% cash.

During the serious market downturn in 2008, I gradually moved to 50% cash because this was an exceptional market condition. Because of my cash position, I was able to buy a good stock at a ridiculously low price and more than tripled my investment in 18 months. I could not have taken this opportunity if I hadn't had some available cash in my account.

Nothing increases your odds of success better than buying good stocks on sale — you need ready cash to do this

But in general, I personally stick with the 10% to 20% level.

So keep some cash in your account. You never know when a quality stock will go on sale and you can make a lot of money.

EXTRA CREDIT JUST FOR FUN: Cash actually seems to have some characteristics of a loan — kind of like a little mini bond without a stated maturity date.

Just think – if you went to your banker to get a $1000 loan to be paid (with interest) in 90 days, he would have you sign a NOTE promising to pay.

Now look at a dollar bill. What does it say? It says Federal

Reserve NOTE. This NOTE is legal tender for all DEBTS, public and private. That sounds like a loan, doesn't it.

Who'd of thought cash might be loaning instead of owning?

EXTRA EXTRA CREDIT: You might have been surprised when I listed cash as an investment. And my statement that it is a poor investment still holds.

But years ago I actually made money on it. I was on assignment in London, traveling back and forth every so often to the United States. So I would buy British pounds before I flew to London.

When I returned, I would take my left over British pound notes to my bank and change them into dollars. During many trips between London and the states I made money, because when I got back to the states, the British pound had become more valuable against the U. S. dollar. So I got more dollars than I had paid originally.

There is an entire field of foreign currency exchange that does this as investment. It's definitely beyond the scope of this book and I don't think falls into the category of beginning investor.

It's just an interesting thought to share.

PART 4: Different Types Of Investments

Money Market

Just think about money market like you think about cash and you'll be fine

Unless you are a BIG investor, don't get hung up on the interest rate money market pays — it won't be very much

You can just think of money market as cash that also earns a little interest. For your purposes, if you have money market funds in your account, you can use them just like cash to buy stocks.

Most online brokers will look through your account every day or so and take any new cash that has been added to it, and turn it into money market funds for you automatically. They do this so you are getting a small interest return on your cash.

This is a nice feature called a sweep, i.e. they are sweeping up your cash. At first you may be confused when you see these money market balances and transactions in your account, but don't let them throw you. They are just automatically doing this service for you.

Also, unless you are a BIG investor, don't get hung up on the interest rate it pays. It won't be much. I've seen some investors focus way too much on this. Remember, you are looking to make significantly more money by focusing on and investing in quality stocks.

Just think of money market like you think about cash and you'll be fine.

EXTRA CREDIT: Do you know what money market funds really are? They are just bonds that are about to come due.

So a money market manager always has bonds that will come due in one day, two days, three days, etc. That way he can get the bond interest for you, but be able to have plenty of cash available for you every day as the bonds expire day by day.

Stock Based Investments

The following are investments within the scope of this book. They all have stocks at their core.

Remember that other types of investments may also fit your unique financial position, but a significant portion of them will probably be stock-based, which is why we focus on them.

Also, to cover every type of investment would be confusing and defeat the purpose of this book. I touch on other investments briefly in the final chapter of this section just for your personal edification, but they are not our focus here.

All that said, we start off with individual stocks.

On average, stocks have returned 8% per year over the long term

Individual Stocks. These are the main investments you will focus on. Stocks are where you buy part ownership in a company. You'll recall we mentioned earlier that you are a true business owner when you buy stocks.

This means you own a portion of the profits the company makes every year. If it is a dividend paying stock, they will pay you these profits in dividends deposited into your trading account. You will literally see your cash balance go up the day they do this. Or you can have them send you a check.

Either way you do it, it's a pretty nice feeling.

Not all stocks pay dividends. They may reinvest the money to grow the business. That's okay too. Because when the business grows, your stocks should eventually become worth more money. And that's why we invest. That's a good feeling too.

The best stock trade I've made in the past two years returned a WHOPPING 1400% in a matter of weeks — I got the idea from one of the newsletters I recommend later in the book

On average, stocks have increased about 8% a year over the long term.

A WHOPPING 1400% STOCK TRADE — IN WEEKS

The best stock trade I've done in the past couple of years was a small junior gold mining stock called ATAC Resources Limited — symbol ATADF.

You can go boom or bust in the junior miners. In this case it was boom — as in sonic boom! The stock went from .25 a share to $8.00 a share in about 19 weeks. *Most of that move occurred in one week. You may guess — correctly — that they hit a rich gold deposit.*

I sold four times my original investment and still own plenty of shares—so I'm playing with house money.

You may hook onto one of these rocket rides yourself someday. I mention the financial newsletter I got the idea from in the section *How Do I Know What Stocks To Buy*.

It's written by a geologist named Matt Badiali, and he's one of my favorite investment newsletter writers (go figure). You might want to pay attention to that section.

Here's the chart of that gold stock rocket ride

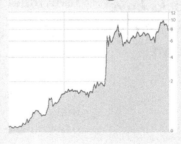

You could buy shares of the top 500 companies individually — or you could buy an index fund that has already done that for you

Index Funds. In this case I mean specifically stock index funds. These are funds that invest in certain groups of stocks for your convenience. For example, maybe you think all of the stocks of the big corporations in the United States are going to go up over time. Maybe you would like to invest in the top 500 companies.

You could go out and buy shares of each of these five hundred companies individually. But that sounds like a lot of work — and commissions, come to think of it.

Or you could buy an index fund that has already done that for you. And they charge a very low fee. I'm warming up to that idea, aren't you?

And nicer still, Index Funds trade just like stocks from your perspective. By that I mean, they have a symbol, and you can

PART 4: Different Types Of Investments

For the most part, I treat Index Funds and Exchange Traded Funds (ETF's) like they are the same

go out and buy them and sell them in seconds, just like you would a regular stock. One of the more widely known index funds like I just described is the S&P 500 index fund, symbol SPC, made up of the top 500 U. S. Corporations.

Exchange Traded Funds (ETF's). I mean specifically stock based ETF's here, as there are ETF's that invest in other things as well. These are similar to index funds in that someone else packages up a bunch of stocks, saving you the trouble of having to go out and buy them all individually.

They also trade like stocks. By that I mean they have a symbol, and you can go out and buy and sell them immediately. So what's the difference between ETF's and Index funds?

For our purposes not much. In general, index funds seem to charge a lower fee. And there are a number of underlying technical differences involving reinvestment of dividends, taxation, etc. But for the most part, I trade them both as if they are the same type of stock-based investment.

A well known ETF, based on the top 500 companies in America, has a symbol of SPY. It is also referred to as the SPDR S&P 500 (Standard & Poor's Depositary Receipt — that really helps—doesn't it?). Some people call them spiders because of the abbreviation.

Stock Mutual Funds. Similar to ETF's and index funds but with a couple of differences. Similar in that they are typically made up of a group of different stocks. Different in that they are actively managed every day, and so the management fee may be a bit higher.

After all, these people don't come to work for free. Also, mutual funds don't trade quite like a stock. They do have a symbol, but you can't buy and sell them instantly.

Typically you have to put your order in to REDEEM them overnight. Also, many of them have a minimum you must invest, like $1000. You can't buy just one share like you can stocks and the other funds mentioned above.

PART 4: Different Types Of Investments

Master Limited Partnerships (MLP's). Don't let the name throw you. I have had great success with some of these and they fit my ownership definition. As a matter of fact, my fantastic investment in Mark West Energy I described earlier was an MLP.

Don't let the name throw you — for our purposes, Master Limited Partnerships (MLP's) trade just like stocks

For your purposes, MLP's trade just like a stock. By that I mean they have a symbol, and you can buy and sell them in seconds – just like a stock.

But they can have really good dividends associated with them. Remember, I was (and still am) getting paid a 20% dividend on the Mark West Energy MLP.

How can they do this? Because they get special treatment from the government. The government will not tax them IF they distribute at least 90% of their dividends to the owners like you and me.

Many of these MLP's are in the energy business. The government gives them this tax break to encourage energy production.

The symbol for Mark West is MWE. But don't be disappointed when you check it out and it's not paying 20% dividends today. It is paying me 20% because I bought it at $13 a share (making our earlier point that it's important to keep some ready cash in your account so you can buy when deals like this come along). The price is considerably higher than that today, so the percent dividend is much lower.

I really like MLP's. I wish there were more of them

You should also note that MLP's are treated differently on your income tax with some fairly complicated rules. I let my tax man deal with that. And I've not seen any big bad tax effect using them. Certainly nothing that outweighs the returns I've made.

I really like MLP's. I wish there were more of them.

EXTRA CREDIT: Why do I say MLP's are like being a business owner? Well, consider this. Stocks are an ownership position in corporations.

But corporations are not the only way businesses are organized. There are also partnerships and single owner

PART 4: Different Types Of Investments

You can invest in precious metals through stocks and ETF's

I believe everyone should have part of their investments in precious metals

Physical silver is so cheap and easy to invest in, even a child can do it — and I know of some who do ... what was that about out of the mouths of babes and words of wisdom

businesses (called sole proprietorships).

So when you buy part of a Master Limited PARTNERSHIP, you are like a limited partner. Sounds like a business owner, doesn't it?

Precious Metals. By precious metals I mean gold and silver. As you saw earlier in our rocket ride gold miner investment, you can invest in precious metals by investing in the stocks of companies that mine and process them. And there are precious metals ETF's you can buy that hold a group of precious metals stocks.

I believe everyone should have some investment in precious metals. How much of your portfolio you invest in them is subject to debate. The general number I hear is 5 to 10%. I currently have 20% because I believe we are headed for hyperinflation as we debase the U.S. Dollar to monetize the debt.

But this is a personal choice you will need to make.

Related to precious metals is buying physical silver. While this is a non-stock investment, it is still an owner position investment you may want to consider.

And it is an easy investment to make. You don't even need a stock account. And you can get started for under $5. That's right. I said "under $5." This is another successful investment I do that has more than doubled in the past year.

And it's so cheap and easy even a child can do it. If you are interested, we have a full report on physical silver at the Live Learn and Prosper site. I've been involved in silver investing since 1979, and believe you will find it well worth the money. You can get the report by going to this link at *Silver Report.*

~~~~~

So that concludes our review of stock-based investments. In the next chapter, we touch on other types of investments just to expose you to them.

Feel free to skip that section if you like and go straight to the ***Let's Get Started*** chapter, where our focus returns to stocks and stock-based investments.

Other Types Of Investments

While not in the scope of this book, listed below are some of the other types of investments. They are not in the scope of this book because they are really quite different from stocks and/or may be advanced beyond Beginning Investment.

Bonds. A bond is simply you loaning money to a corporation for a certain period of time, so they will pay you interest. For example, you might buy a ten year bond for $1000 that pays 5% interest. When you buy the bond, you have loaned that money to the corporation.

Many people mistakenly believe that they can't lose the original $1000 bond investment they made, but that is only true if you hold it to it's maturity date (in this example 10 years).

Many people don't realize that the value of a bond can go up and down just like stocks

The price and value of a bond goes up and down just like the price and value of stocks in the stock market. So if you bought a ten year bond, and decided to sell it a year later, it may only be worth $600 — or it may be worth $1200 — all depending on current interest rates and how badly people want to buy your bond.

Why is that, you may wonder. Well, if interest rates went up and the company issued some more bonds that paid 10% interest, everyone would want to buy the new bonds because they paid twice as much interest. Remember, the bond you bought and own only pays 5%. So they won't be interested in buying your bond for the full $1000 you paid because they can get a much better deal today. So they will offer much less than $1000 to buy your bond.

I'm not against bonds as investments — they just aren't in the scope of this book

Bonds are typically a little more difficult to buy than stocks where you can place a buy and sell order and have it execute in seconds and begin to see results immediately. For this reason and others, they are not in the scope of this book.

Indeed, some corporate bonds do incredibly well. But you have to have good research to buy the right ones at a deep discount

I'm not against bonds if they are done correctly. Indeed, one of the financial newsletters I read does incredibly well with them by buying them at deep discounts.

But most people don't buy with this kind of research. They

PART 4: Different Types Of Investments

Certificates of Deposit (CD's) are similar to bonds in that you are LOANING money — typically to a bank

Likewise, U. S. Treasury Notes / Bonds are when you are loaning money to the Federal government ... they seem to need quite a bit of that these days

If you get nothing else out of the commodities section, learn that cocoa pods are commodities and this is what chocolate is made out of. What could be more important than that?

just mistakenly buy them assuming they are safe investments, and this is not always the case.

Certificates of Deposit (CD's). CD's are similar to bonds in that you are loaning money to an organization (often a bank) so they will pay you interest. CD's are not in the scope of this book.

You can cash in your CD's any time and get the full face value less a hefty early withdrawal penalty for doing so. This can defeat the purpose of investing in them.

Also, CD's often pay an interest rate that is lower than inflation, so you are actually losing purchasing power while you hold them.

Commodity Futures and Options. Commodities are basic agricultural products and materials we all depend on. Some examples are corn, wheat, soybeans, coffee, sugar, oil, copper, cattle, hogs and pork bellies, to name a few.

And cocoa pods, the agricultural product that chocolate is made out of. That makes it the most important commodity of the bunch, don't you agree?

There is a huge commodity market in the United States, sixteen times the size of the stock market, that trades in these necessary goods. And large sums of money can be made (and lost) quickly trading them as futures contracts or options.

It takes some real trading expertise and nerves of steel to invest in these successfully. I've read that only 5% of the traders make money, which means the other 95% lose. And most new traders blow up their account (as in lose ALL their money) within the first year.

I started trading them in the early 90's and did not blow up any of my accounts, but can attest to the nerves of steel thing (my trading partner nicknamed me Steely Dan).

Suffice it to say we will not be getting into commodities in this book. There are many profitable opportunities in stocks that will go much easier on your nerves.

WHAT ARE PORK BELLIES?

Have you ever wondered what pork bellies are? It's kind of a funny name for an investment, isn't it? Before I got into commodities I used to hear about them and wonder what they were.

Pork bellies are the underside of a pig — the right and left side of the belly. They are what bacon is made out of.

And they are serious business. If you own a contract of bellies and the price goes up just $1 a pound you make $400. Of course, if it goes down $1 a pound you lose $400. Wow. That's some kind of leverage, wouldn't you say?

Below is a picture of a pork belly. Looks kind of like bacon, doesn't it? Because that's what they make bacon out of. Now you know.

CRUDE OIL SPECULATORS

If you think the pork bellies are highly leveraged investments, try crude oil on for size. If you own a contract of crude oil and the price goes up $1 a barrel, you make a thousand dollars.

Gee, I wonder why there are so many oil speculators out there. And yes, I've traded crude oil, so I've been an evil oil speculator myself (reformed).

But it's a completely open market. Anyone can set up a commodities account and start trading crude oil. But the prices can swing wildly and are hard to predict due to politicians, countries, world events and disasters. So I'll say not recommended if you want to sleep at night. Stock investing should be looking pretty good to you about now.

PART 4: Different Types Of Investments

Currencies. There is a huge currency market that trades around the world, 24 hours a day, 7 days a week, where people buy and sell the different country currencies, like the Swiss Franc, U.S. Dollars, British Pound, Mexican Peso, etc.

They are mainly traded on the FOREX market, although some of them are also traded on the commodities market. This is another one of those "nerves of steel" trades where fortunes can be made and lost rapidly.

Currency trading can be highly influenced by the various countries and the actions of their politicians. That pretty much does it for me ... I stay away from them

I've read it takes ten years of study to actually be able to trade these well. And outside of my inadvertent currency trades with British Pounds when I was traveling to England for an extended period of time, I've not invested in them.

They can be highly influenced by the various countries and actions of their politicians. That pretty much says it all for me. We'll stay away from country currencies.

Other Investments. Of course there are many other types of investments you can make. Like real estate, the investment that everyone thought would never go down — that is until around 2008. And fine art, rare coins, etc.

But enough of understanding the basics. We'll stick with stocks and move on to the next section. It's time to do something. It's time to get started and open a stock market account.

PART 5: Let's Get Started

Opening A Stock Market Account

What Is A Stock Market Account?

Choosing A Broker

Setting Up An Account

What Is A Stock Market Account?

Just about everyone has a checking account at their bank. You have to open a checking account before you can make deposits, write checks and earn interest.

Just like you have to open a checking account to do your banking, you have to open a stock market account to do your trading

Similarly, you have to open a stock market account before you can make deposits, buy stocks and get dividends. So you can think of your stock market account as your checking account for stocks.

Except instead of just having cash in it, it has cash and stocks and other investments in it that you own. And just like you can look at your checking account online and see all your deposits, withdrawals and balance, you can look at you stock market account.

The top part of the screen will look something like this.

Balances & Positions	Balance($)	Today's Net Change
Cash Balance	5700	0
Long Stock Value	*4300*	*85*
Account Value	10000	85

Remember, the word "Long" just means you own the shares

Balance ($) on the Cash Balance line shows that you have $5700 in cash in your account. You can use this to buy other stocks if you want.

Today's Net Change on the cash balance line is $0. That means you did not buy any stocks today, you did not make any deposits, and you did not receive any dividends from your stocks.

These two sentences mean exactly the same thing ...
1) *I OWN 10 shares of Sprint stock*
2) *I am LONG 10 shares of Sprint stock*

Balance ($) on the Long Stock Value line shows that you own stocks in your account that are valued at $4300 at this moment. Remember the word long just means you own these shares (see *What Does Long And Short Mean*).

And **Today's Net Change** on the Long Stock Value line shows that the value of your stocks and your account went up by $85 today, even though you didn't do anything — not bad.

So the **Balance ($)** on the Account Value line shows your total account is $10,000 right now. This would be like your checking account balance.

And **Today's Net Change** on the Account Value line shows that in total, with all your stocks and transactions today, your account went up by $85.

Now lets look at the bottom section. This tells you how each one of the stocks you own is doing. We'll just look at the first line because it's the same thing for all of them.

Symbol	Description	Qty	Purchase Price	Cost	Market Value	Gain($)	Day Gain($)
S	SPRINT	100	5	500	600	100	-10
XOM	EXXON MOBIL CORP	10	82	820	700	-120	10
MCD	MCDONALDS CORP	10	85	850	900	50	25
WMT	WALMART STORES INC	20	53	1060	1200	140	50
FVITF	FORTUNA SILVER MINES	50	5	250	300	50	-10
MOO	MARKET VECTORS AGRIBUSINESS	10	50	500	600	100	20
				3980	**4300**	320	**85**

You remember the word "Symbol," right? Every stock has a unique abbreviation called a symbol

Symbol. You remember this, right? Every stock has a unique abbreviation. So that's what this is. The abbreviation for the stock you own. In this case it is Sprint, the telephone company.

Description spells out the name of the stock symbol so you don't have to remember them, so in this case it says Sprint.

Qty is the quantity, or number of shares you own of this stock. You own 100 shares of Sprint stock.

Purchase Price is how much you paid for each share of Sprint stock when you bought them. You bought your Sprint stock for $5 a share.

Cost is the total amount you paid to buy all of those Sprint shares. Since you bought 100 shares at $5 a share, your cost was $500.

Market Value is how much all those 100 shares are worth

right now. So even though you only paid $500 for them, you could sell them right now for $600. Nice. This is why we invest.

Gain($) is how much money you've made (or lost) on your stock since you bought it — if you sold it right now — today

Gain($) is how much money you have made on your Sprint stock <u>since you first bought it</u> if you sold it right now. Since your cost was $500 and you could sell it for $600, you have gained $100 dollars. This is your profit. Not bad.

Day Gain($) shows how your Sprint stock <u>did today</u> in the stock market. Your total Sprint value went down $10 today. Well, okay, stocks go up and stocks go down day by day.

Day Gain($) means how much money you've made (or lost) on your stock in the market today

Tomorrow, your Sprint shares may be up $20 – or down another $5 or $10. But in total right now you are still $100 ahead in your Sprint stock, so things are okay.

And if you follow the guidelines in this book, you will improve your odds that your gains will be greater than your losses over time.

So that's what your stock market account is, and what it will look like. Every day the values will change based on the stock market.

ABOUT WITHDRAWALS

We started out this chapter relating your stock market account to your checking account. Just like you can make withdrawals from your checking account, you can make withdrawals from your stock market account.

But they are a little slower – my experience has been it takes up to six business days. And the form you need to use is somewhat more complicated than writing out a check at your bank.

Outside of that, they work about the same.

Choosing A Broker

You will need a broker to do the trading described in this book. You have a choice here.

If you use a broker to do your buying and selling, you have the assurance a professional is doing this for you

You can pay a broker to do your buying and selling for you. Your advantage is you will not have to learn how to place buy and sell orders, and you will have the assurance a professional is doing this for you. Of course, brokers have to eat, so they will charge you for this service.

Or you can open an online discount broker account and do all of your trading yourself. While that option is not free, as the name implies, the fees for trading your online account run at a discount to having a broker do the trades for you.

Some people start by using a broker and then move on to trading their own online account

Some people start by using a broker, then move on to trading their own online account. Or you can start right off with an online account. It depends on your level of confidence.

But millions of people trade online today, so it is not terribly difficult if you apply what you learn here. And most discount online brokers give you the option of talking to one of their live brokers to help you through a transaction if you get confused. They will charge you extra for that transaction, but you can watch and learn and do it yourself next time at the online discount fee.

Millions of people trade online today, so it's not terribly difficult if you apply what you learn here

While the rest of this book is oriented toward you doing your trading with an online account, all of the information is just as valuable to you if you are using a broker. You will be able to communicate well and understand what they are telling you.

One final thought on brokers before we move on to online trading. Since I used to be one, I can tell you what to look for. There are many good and conscientious brokers out there. A good broker should be accessible to you, return your calls, periodically keep you up to date on the status of your account, and they should take the time to explain any transactions that you don't understand.

Of course, brokers are busy like the rest of us, so unless you have good reason, you shouldn't be calling them every five minutes — just when you need to.

What to look out for with a broker — well, unless you are a frequent, high volume trader, they should not be calling you constantly trying to get you to buy and sell stocks (unless there is an extraordinary market condition like the bear market in 2008).

Since they are commission based, if you sense your broker is constantly trying to generate trading activity with you, think about getting another broker. That said, there are many conscientious brokers out there so don't let that last comment throw you.

Now to the online discount broker approach. If you are going to take this route, and there is no reason why most of you shouldn't, here are some thoughts on choosing one.

There are online discount brokers and super discount brokers.

I go for the run of the mill discount brokers and pass on the super discount brokers

There are online discount brokers and super discount brokers. I had trouble with a super discount broker in my commodity options trading past, so I avoid the super discount guys, and go for the more run of the mill discount brokers.

Some brokers that fit this description and are competitors with each other are …

- TDAmeritrade
- Scottrade
- E*Trade
- Fidelity Investments
- Charles Schwab

Setting up and keeping an account with these brokers should be free and the cost per trade (when you buy or sell a stock) should be around $10. Some will be more, some less.

For example, I recently saw a television commercial for Scottrade advertising $7 per trade. Since you probably wont be trading that much, a few dollars more or less is probably not that big of an issue. I tend to choose these things based more on ease of use.

Typically you will not be trading a great deal, so your number of trade transactions may range from none to no more than five or ten in some months. (and that's kind of high, actually).

Note that I said typically here. I may have had forty trades in one month during the peak of the market problems in 2008 – but that is not typical.

Another consideration is if you work in an office during the day and want to occasionally check on your stocks through your employer's computer. You will want to make sure the broker you chose can be accessed through your companies' firewall.

If you can't decide on a discount broker, here's a helpful hint. I have been very satisfied using TDAmeritrade for years

I can tell you from personal experience that TDAmeritrade works fine through the firewalls of companies I've worked at in the past, and I have read that Scottrade is set up this way as well.

The others listed above may very well work too, but you will want to verify this up front with them when you are setting up your stock account.

I have used TDAmeritrade for over eight years and been very satisfied with them. They are responsive in case I need to call them – which is rare – and I have recommended them to my friends.

Online broker responsiveness is particularly important to you for two reasons.

The first reason involves setting up your account to get started. Since this requires filling out numerous forms, possibly transferring old 401k plans, and even writing out a check in a certain specific way, it's important to know you can call them to walk you through the process.

Fortunately, you only have to do this once to get started.

The second reason is when you want to put on your first trade. If you are not totally comfortable with this, it's probably a good idea to have them walk you through that process.

I would emphasize this point for the first time you sell a stock because you don't want to accidently sell more than you own. Then you will be short the extra shares. This leaves you with a potentially large financial exposure.

It's theoretically unlimited. Which means not only could you lose your entire investment, but your house, car and everything else. Don't let that scare you off. It's pretty straight forward — just be careful and have them walk you through the process the first time if it looks confusing to you.

Just stick to a basic trading platform ... you don't need one with all the dials, levers, flashing lights and gizmos

One other point is that you only need their basic trading platform. Many of them offer super trading platforms that have more dials, levers, flashing lights and gizmos than you can imagine. There is usually an extra charge for these unless you have an account valued over some limit like $25,000.

To my way of thinking this is all unnecessary and is simply paying extra money for unneeded complexity.

Just keep it simple with basic trades. The keys to success in this book focus much more on getting quality, easy to understand research on what to buy and sell, and doing this in a deliberate manner, rather than trying to be Super Joe Day Trader twisting all the knobs and dials on a complex online screen.

So that's it on selecting an online discount broker. Once you have bought and sold a few stocks you will start to feel comfortable with the process.

It's actually quite fun and empowering, in that you are affecting a transaction real time in the world market.

Setting Up An Account

Before calling to set up an account, gather up any 401k or other investment statements and your check book - you'll need information from these—like your bank routing code and account number

Once you have decided on an online broker you will need to set up your stock account with them.

Before you call you will want to gather up any papers you may need. For example, if you are transferring a 401k from a place of previous employment to start your account, you will want to have one of your statements handy. They will need information from it to walk you through a transfer request form.

Or if you are starting it by mailing them a check, or wiring funds from your checking account, they will need the account number and bank routing code. Same deal if you intend for them to make regular deposits from your checking account into your stock account. So one way or another, you need to have your checkbook out.

Once you've gathered all of this information, then give them a call and have them walk you through the process.

Here's a big clue ... setting up a new account should be free, and they should be very helpful ... if not, I'd choose another broker

Here's a big clue for you. They should be very helpful with this process. If they are not, then politely end the phone conversation and pick another discount broker.

My experience with TDAmeritrade, as well as some of my friends, has been quite satisfactory. So if none of the other brokers seem to help out, you might call them.

Discount Broker Web Sites

Here are links to the discount brokers mentioned earlier in the chapter.

TDAmeritrade
www.tdameritrade.com

Scottrade
www.scottrade.com

E*Trade
www.etrade.com

PART 5: Let's Get Started

Fidelity Investments
www.fidelity.com

Charles Schwab
www.schwab.com

PART 6: Choosing And Buying Good Stocks

How Do I Know What Stocks To Buy?

Sample Newsletter

My Favorite Newsletters

Pick And Buy Using A Warren Buffett Mindset

Placing A Buy Order

How Do I Know What Stocks To Buy?

Remember when you are buying a stock you are buying a business

Remember that when you invest in a stock, you are buying a business. You are becoming a business owner.

No smart business person would buy a business without doing some serious research first.

They would want to know what the sales were, if the sales were increasing every year, how much profit those sales were creating, if profits were increasing every year, if the company was badly in debt, and many other things.

You need to know this too before you buy a stock.

No serious business person would buy a business without research

Don't get discouraged about all this research because there is an easy way to get this done for you. Let someone else do it. This is what I do.

I don't have hours per week to spend researching the companies I want to invest in, so I get the advice of people who do this for a living.

I don't have hours per week to do research, so I let someone else do it for me

There are two ways to get this advice. One way is free and one way you have to pay for. I use the paid way, but I list a couple of free sources later in this chapter.

Before you immediately rule out paying for advice, here are a couple of things to consider. One is that you would be surprised at the low price of some great quality investment newsletters and what a terrific value they are for the money. I typically buy newsletters that cost $89 per year, and often they are on sale for $39 per year if you catch their specials. That's about eight lattes per year at Starbucks, and these newsletters can make you some of the other kind of bucks.

Remember, I was a financial consultant and a New York Stock Exchange licensed broker. I could do some of this research myself. And I had all kinds of free company research available to me. And I still bought these newsletters.

In my opinion, they are that good and worth every penny.

So I take the easy road and buy specific newsletters. I make ALL of my investments based on their recommendations.

The second consideration is that free advice is often worth what you pay for it. Your money is at stake here so this may not be the time to be cheap.

Free Trade Sources

That said, lets get the free sources out of the way first and then move on to the paid sources. Full disclosure here: I do not use these two sources, but watch them and go to their sites on occasion.

The first is Jim Cramer who has a nightly television show on CNBC called Mad Money. I like him and watch him frequently. Be warned — he is a pretty animated character. Personally, I think he should never drink coffee. But I like him just the same.

And he has been a very successful investor. Also, he gives specific stock recommendations, and he is good at explaining things.

I have read his book ***Getting Back To Even – Your Personal Economic Recovery Plan,*** and it's quite good. I recommend it for those who want to get much deeper into the subject of stock investments.

Jim has quite a following and so you don't have to watch his show every night to get his recommendations. There are a number of web sites that publish them.

Here is one that you can check out at http://www.cramers-mad-money.com/.

The other show I watch often, also on CNBC, is Fast Money, hosted by Melissa Lee. Who doesn't like watching Melissa? She moderates a panel of four other traders who discuss stocks, and at the end of the show, she asks each one of them for a specific trade they would recommend.

These tips are also posted on their web site, so you don't need to watch the show every evening to keep up.

You can see their site and recommendations at http://www.cnbc.com/id/17390482, or in case this changes, just

Recommendations from both these financial shows are posted on the internet so you don't have to watch the shows every night

PART 6: Choosing And Buying Good Stocks

Google "Fast Money Final Trade" to see their latest recommendations.

That said, I use neither of these sources to pick trades. By their nature, newsletters give you a more thorough and deliberate analysis. And they follow up with the status of their picks. Many also send you email alerts when something unusual has happened, or it is time to sell.

I would treat the two free sources as great education—and entertainment. After all, there's nothing wrong with having fun while you learn.

There are a lot of knock-off newsletters out there that aren't so good ... if you can't decide, then check out some I list and use

But for my money, I go with the paid financial newsletters — every time.

There are many knock off newsletters out there that are not good, so I go into detail reviewing the ones I have had good success with. You might want to consider some of them too.

But before we get into the specific newsletters, lets look at a sample one to get started. A good newsletter has certain characteristics which I will point out.

One of the characteristics I look for will give you the ability to just scan it rapidly and make a decision — or to read it in depth. You decide.

Paid Trade Sources

The typical newsletter price I pay is around $60 to $89 per year — and sometimes they are on sale for $39

Financial newsletters can cost anywhere from $39 per year up to $25,000 and more per year. We will be avoiding the $25,000 per year variety. The typical newsletter price I pay is around $60 to $89 per year. If you subscribe for two years, that price can come down by a third. And once you have bought one of the newsletters they will have you on their list and probably make you some of the discounted $39 offers in the future.

And you really only need one to be successful, although I think you will probably wind up buying two or three eventually because they are so good.

As I mentioned earlier, I choose newsletters that follow a

specific format. This format is good for me, and it will be good for you as a beginning investor.

The newsletters I buy always tell a story about the recommendations they are making for the month. They describe the research they did and their reasoning for the positive future financial prospects of the business.

I choose newsletters that follow a SPECIFIC format. They tell a story, describe their research and then end with a SPECIFIC buy statement ... like Buy Sprint up to $5 a share

And they end the article with a specific buy statement that looks like this. Example*: **Buy Sprint NYSE: S up to $5 a share and use a 25% trailing stop.***

Here's why this is good for you as a beginning investor. Even if you don't understand all the business talk and research they describe in the story, you will know exactly what to buy at what price to take advantage of their recommendation.

See what they said in the example above about Sprint. They told you to buy Sprint stock. They told you to not buy it for more than $5 a share. And they even told you the Stock symbol — which is "S" — to enter into the screen when you place your order in your online stock account.

What could be easier? Really?

They don't waffle about this or hedge their bets

If you are one of those people that skips to the end of a book to find out the ending, you could do the same here -- decide how many shares you wanted to buy and place the order.

I don't recommend that because I think you will begin to learn more about stocks as you read the stories. Even if you don't get the whole thing, you will form an impression and get a feel for what they are talking about.

I have friends who don't know anything about stocks – but have been interested in their investments – that I have shared some stock stories with, and they read them from top to bottom.

They might not understand the whole thing, but they get the general idea. You will too.

It gets better yet. Because when you buy one of these special newsletters I describe below, they will send you a special alert if the stock starts going bad.

PART 6: Choosing And Buying Good Stocks

So they do all the business research for you (saving you hours of hard work). And they have successful track records. They tell you exactly what to buy and how much to pay. And they tell you when to get out.

Also, at the end of the newsletter, they have a list of all of their current recommendations, how they are doing, which ones you can still buy if you like, and the maximum price you should pay for them.

That pretty much covers everything you need to know, right?

I think you will agree this is so much better than Uncle Harry's stock tip he tells you about at Thanksgiving after he's had a couple of drinks.

I think you'll agree this is better than Uncle Harry's stock tip he gives you at Thanksgiving after he's had a few drinks

Or the hot stock tip your buddy tells you about. Or the hot stock tip on the evening news. By the way, I've heard some of these newscasters can't even balance their expense accounts. And they are reporting hot stock tips? Interesting.

One final point. Even when I was a stockbroker, with all the research of a major U. S. broker/dealer at my fingertips, I read these newsletters.

So let's look at a sample newsletter that fits my specifications. Then I will tell you some specific newsletters that I have had success with over the years.

PART 6: Choosing And Buying Good Stocks

Sample Newsletter

Below is a sample newsletter I paraphrased to illustrate all the key points I look for. Please note that the newsletter is a mockup, and the companies are fictitious, so don't place a trade based on this example.

Penny Stock Demo Newsletter
July, 2011

Finding Safe, High Potential Stocks Around the World
Recently, one of my favorite rules was confirmed yet again in the stock market. Technology stock XYZ, a popular favorite, was riding high, up 110% from two years ago. It is what I call a high expectation stock.

The story is good to read, but you don't have to ...

Because of its popularity with the public, it was very expensive. It never ceases to amaze me that the crowd of investors only gets interested in buying stocks when they are high and overpriced. Whatever happened to the concept of buying things on sale?

These stocks always eventually get crushed, along with their investors. Sure enough, XYZ started taking a swan dive two months ago and has lost over half of its value. So all the eager investors at the top have taken huge losses. So much for high expectation stocks.

I learned long ago to look for just the opposite, what I call low expectation stocks. For example, in my last issue, I listed a number of low expectation stocks like Office Maxx and BankZ. They were at the lowest price in twenty years and well worth more than the market was willing to pay. After all, with the economy worried about a possible second depression, who would want to buy an office supply or banking stock?

But this is just when and where we can pick up incredible values. I'm talking stocks that have a potential to rocket up

400 to 800% in twelve months. I have seen this happen time and again. These are low expectation stocks. They are low and unloved by the public. They are the epitome of what Warren Buffett is talking about when he says, "Be greedy when others are fearful."

These stocks are among the safest, highest-performing stocks you can buy. When low-expectation stocks do something wrong, the shares won't fall much. But when they do something right, *shares can soar*.

This Month's Recommendation

This month my recommendation is just such a low expectation, high value stock. The company I am talking about is SprintFast, the communications service company. It is a top brand name under $10 a share, so it fits our Penny Stock profile.

SprintFast provides cell phone and telephone services to roughly 50 million people around the world — mostly in the U.S. It has a market cap of $9.7 billion and revenue of $33.6 billion over the last 12 months.

Its services include local and long distance calling as well as voicemail and internet access. Customers can get the services by long term contracts or pay as they go. Last year the customers averaged spending $59 per month.

SprintFast Has Had Its Share of Problems

SprintFast has been part of a number of mergers that have not yielded the synergy and economies of scale expected. Additionally, the mergers have caused complication and confusion with its customer base.

So business started to fall apart. To compound the problems, the company faced a steep debt service burden from its acquisition costs. And to make matters worse, executives of the newly merged company were at odds with each other.

Things got so bad the company lost 80% of its value.

But these problems that dragged down SprintFast's stock price no longer exist.

They have been focusing on their customer service and aggressively paying down debt. And reorganization has eliminated the internal executive squabbling.

Reasons Shares Are Headed Higher
Earlier in the year, SprintFast did not have any significant products to launch. But now they have the SuperPhone and the SuperDuperPhone, both rolled out three months ago. Both of these phones have been certified to be more reliable than competitor's offerings and have triple the battery life.

Last quarter, SprintFast sold more than 820,000 of these devices and the forecast is to quadruple these sales by the end of the year.

With the huge customer loyalty of their remaining base, slowing of customer outflows and a high level of prepaid subscribers, this unloved, undervalued, low expectation stock is set to soar like an eagle.

Right now, SprintFast trades at an 80% discount to book

PART 6: Choosing And Buying Good Stocks

value and just 4 times earnings before interest, taxes, depreciation, and amortization (EBITDA). This is a steep discount to the industry average of over five times EBITDA.

(**Note:** EBITDA is usually a better proxy than actual earnings when comparing valuations between companies. It excludes tax rates and interest, which can sometimes be volatile for each company quarter to quarter.)

This favorable risk/reward is what we look for in under $10 stocks.

Must read – here's where they tell you exactly what to do

Action to take: Buy SprintFast Nextel (S: NYSE) up to $5.75 a share. Place a 25% trailing stop on your position.

The Penny Stock Demo Model Portfolio

Company	Symbol	Ref Price	Ref Date	Recent Price	Total Return	Status	Description
Royal Gold	RGLD	$38	5/21/10	$80	128%	Buy below $66	Gold Processor
SprintFast	S	$5	5/30/11	$10	100%	Buy below $8	Phone Co
Chesapeake	CHK	$28	6/1/11	$31	10%	Buy below $25	Natural Gas
Wal-Mart	WMT	$40	1/1/09	$50	20%	Buy below $46	Retail

So the sample newsletter you read has all of the components I look for. It has a story, the recent company performance and the researcher's rational for why it should do well in the future.

Then they end with a specific buy recommendation. And at the end of the newsletter you can review all of their active recommendations in case some of these might interest you too.

Now let's look at some of my favorite newsletters. I've done well with them, and you can too.

PART 6: Choosing And Buying Good Stocks

My Favorite Newsletters

In my opinion these guys are some of the rock stars of the financial newsletter industry

Porter Stansberry

Dan Ferris

Matt Badiali

Frank Curzio

Here are some of the newsletters I've used off and on through the years. In my opinion, these guys are some of the rock stars of the financial newsletter business.

I'm sure there are many other good ones, but it would be impossible to research them all. Of course, you will have to decide which recommendations work well for you and your specific circumstances. But these have worked well for me, so I'll share them with you, along with some of my comments.

Extreme Value. This is a monthly investment research service written by Dan Ferris, one of the best financial analysts in the country. I really like Dan and his newsletter. He has a real straight-talking style and his recommendations seem well thought out and researched.

He focuses on value investing – recommending stocks of quality companies trading at big discounts to their true value.

When you buy quality stocks at a big discount you greatly increase your odds of success. This in turn lowers your risk of loss because the stock was already down when you bought it. Here's a short excerpt and pretty impressive statistic from their marketing material.

"Not only are Extreme Value stocks profitable, they are also the safest you can own. The strategy Dan uses has been proven to beat the overall market in a 27-year study by two University of Chicago professors (one of whom was nominated for a Nobel Prize). "

"Extreme Value stocks are founded on the classic value investing ideas of Benjamin Graham and Warren Buffett. Simply put: The method Dan uses to pick stocks is time-tested. And historically, these are the safest and best-performing stocks of all."

You can't go far wrong following Dan and his newsletter, if you ask me.

The S&A Resource Report. I find this to be an exciting monthly newsletter written by Matt Badiali. It's about natural resource investments such as oil, natural gas and precious metals.

Some of my favorite recommendations have been in gold and silver processing, mining and exploration. They almost make you feel like you are a prospector – but without all the physical labor.

More importantly, I've done well with a number of his recommendations in gold, silver and oil. *Matt recommended ATAC Resources, the small Yukon gold miner I made 1400% on in a matter of weeks. That should get your attention.*

Matt Badiali recommended ATAC Resources, the small Yukon gold miner I made 1400% on in a matter of weeks

Matt literally fly's around the world searching out the best resource investments. He's well qualified to do so with more than 15 years of experience as a hydrologist, geologist, and a consultant to the oil industry.

He holds a masters degree in geology from Florida Atlantic University and is currently pursuing his Ph.D. in the same field at the University of North Carolina. But all qualifications aside, it's the results that he gets that I like.

Here's what they say about his success and results.

"Matt's recommendations in the S&A Resource Report have shown subscribers significant gains, including Petrobras (165%), Stone Energy (93%), Veritas (77%), and recently Parker Drilling (77%). "

"Here at Stansberry & Associates Investment Research, we believe the global economy is still in the grip of a long-term bull market for oil, precious metals, and other natural resources the likes of which the world has never seen. Demand is going through the roof, and one of the best places investors can have their money over the next few years is in oil, energy, and mining investments."

Penny Stock Specialist. Penny stocks are small company stocks usually under $10 a share. Some of these companies may be the giants of tomorrow and you can hitch a real rocket ride if you get the right one. But you have to pick based on serious research because there can be a lot of flim-flam to get through in the penny stock world.

PART 6: Choosing And Buying Good Stocks

Penny Stock Specialist solves that for you as one of the world's top penny stock advisories. Editor Frank Curzio is one of America's most recognized experts in this sector.

Also, most stocks in this sector are totally unknown to Wall Street and Main Street alike, which can give you and me a tremendous advantage in the market — with Frank's help, that is.

Frank is a well-connected stock insider who has presented his research on national television - on programs like CNBC's *The Kudlow Report*, CNBC's *The Call*, CNN Radio, and Fox Business News.

Here's what they say about Frank.

"The newsletter is published every two weeks, and provides recommendations readers can expect to hold for 2-12 months. Using a handful of unique methodologies, Frank has compiled one of the best track records in the industry over the past three years, with over 90% of his picks turning a profit, including four stocks that gained over 125%."

Most penny stocks are totally unknown to Wall Street ... giving you and me a tremendous advantage in the market — with Frank Curzio's research help, that is

What's not to like about that? I've invested in a number of penny stocks and think they are well worth looking at as part of your investment portfolio.

Stansberry's Investment Advisory. Written by Porter Stansberry, I really like the overall balance and in-depth research and rationale he uses in his Investment Advisory every month. Porter believes most people take too much risk with their money and recommends they put the majority of their money into his "No Risk" stocks – and hold on to them for many, many years.

But don't get the idea his stock picks are yawn-wide boring. As an aside, and to give you an example, one of them I've invested in is a silver processor — Silver Wheaton (SLW).

Can you guess what they do? Well, gold companies often have left over ore that contains silver. They don't want to mess with it. So Silver Wheaton offers to take it off their hands for them and extracts the silver. They give a portion of the silver back to the gold company and keep the rest. What a business model — taking that pesky silver ore off those gold miners hands for them.

Nothing boring about that recommendation—rather inspired, actually. Where have you heard of an investment like that?

Porter's newsletter comes out monthly and he breaks his stocks out into three investment types. They are 1) "No Risk" stocks that represent ultra-safe, long-term investments 2) "Next Boom" recommendations that feature undervalued stocks poised for growth, and 3) "Forever" stocks that are cheap blue-chips which will provide excellent returns… forever.

I read anything written by Porter Stansberry — he's that good

Here's what they say about Porters results.

"Porter has shown his subscribers some spectacular gains in the past few years, such as 133% on Intuitive Surgical, 233% on Celgene, 215% on ID Biomedical, and 206% on Elan."

Porter also writes many articles about world events that shape the market and you will learn from him. Personally, I read anything he writes. He's that good. So you might want to put him at the top of your newsletter shopping list.

Which leads to—the newsletter shopping list. I've used many more newsletters than I've listed above, but it would take too long to describe them all. So I've provided a link to their entire product line.

I have always been satisfied with their products. And I've even met some of the writers in person in Delray Beach, Florida.

So you might want to look into their subscriptions. Because well researched stock picks from quality newsletters like these are a MAJOR factor in your investment success. You can check them out here at http://www.stansberryresearch.com/pub/btr/index.asp

Pick And Buy Using A Warren Buffett Mindset

So we finally get to the point of picking and buying a good stock. How do we do that?

First, start by reading your newsletter(s). Read a story and see if it makes sense to you. Does it seem this stock has a good reason to go up? Are you pretty enthused by the stock – maybe even a bit excited?

That's good. This may be one you want to invest in. If the story doesn't move you, then just walk away from it. You don't have to invest in it. There is no rush to put on a trade.

But if you like the story and have real enthusiasm for it, that's very good. Because this enthusiasm will carry you through some of the times when it is down—and all stocks go up and down.

Now we get to the recommendation. Here's what it should look like.

Buy SprintFast NYSE:S up to $5 a share and use a 25% trailing stop.

We place our order with a tough minded buying mindset that says if the market doesn't come to us and our price — we don't care — we will not buy

Now take all of that enthusiasm and set it aside. We are going into the tough minded buying mindset—what I like to call the "Warren Buffett mindset."

This means we are not going to pay one more penny over $5 for this stock, no matter how much we like it. If the market price right now is $5.50, we are going to make the market come to us. And if it doesn't—WE DON'T CARE! We won't buy the stock.

You see, Warren Buffett isn't desperate or eager. He doesn't have to be — he has his billions. So he picks and chooses what will be a good deal for him and makes the market come to him — if not, he doesn't buy.

He knows that buying stocks at a low price GREATLY

PART 6: Choosing And Buying Good Stocks

Buying stocks at a low price GREATLY increases your odds of success and lowers your risk

increases your odds of success and lowers your risk.

Think about it this way. If you just had one little stock idea, and that's all you had in the world, you'd be in a mindset to buy—maybe at any price. And that's a recipe for failure.

But you're in a much better position now because you have a steady stream of great, well-researched stock ideas at low prices coming your way every month in your newsletters.

No need to be desperate. Just like catching the bus—if you miss this one, another one will be along in a few minutes. No worries. You don't care.

Also, you've paid for the research which tells you what the maximum price should be. So if you're paying for the research, it's good to use it correctly, right? So don't buy over the "buy up to" price on any of your stocks.

This "buying attitude thing" is one of the most critical factors for your success

Put on a billionaire's "don't care — make it come to me" attitude. Now that you've got the right attitude, it's time to go place an order for your stock pick. Notice I didn't say buy. We don't care if we buy or not. We're just going to put the order out there at the right price and see if the market will come to us — on our terms.

By the way, I realize this "buying attitude thing" is simple, but it "ain't easy." But you'll want to get used to it because I carry it to the EXTREME in the next book, _**Beyond Stock Investing For Beginners**_.

It is one of the most critical factors for your success.

Placing A Buy Order

So if you were going to buy a new pair of slacks or a dress, you would first go to the store and find out the price. If the price was not too high, you would go ahead and make your purchase.

It's the same way with buying a stock. You need to find out the price and make sure it's not too high before you buy. To do this, log in to your stock account and then click on the tabs Research and Ideas —>Stocks.

To check on your stocks, log in to your account, then click tabs Accounts —> Balances & Positions

This will show you a screen like the one below.

Let's say you want to buy stock in Sprint. If you know the symbol is S, then enter S in the search box and click the Go button.

If you don't know the symbol, you can enter "Sprint" in the search box and click on the Symbol Lookup button. This will list all the stocks that have Sprint in their name and what their symbols are. Pick the symbol for the one that is Sprint, enter it into the search box and click the Go button. You will see something like this:

So what does this tell us?

First, the full company name of Sprint, which is Sprint Nextel Corp.

Also that it is a communications company, and (shown in light grey) that it is traded on the New York Stock Exchange (NYSE).

To the right, it shows a little chart of how the stock has been going up and down over the past months. It looks like the overall trend is up, but the current price is down.

That's encouraging — you will be able to buy it at the lower price that it is today. And most important, below the Buy and Sell buttons, is the price($5.17) per share you can buy it right now.

So here's the deal. If your newsletter recommendation said "Buy Sprint NYSE S up to $5.50," should you go ahead and buy the stock?

If your newsletter says buy Sprint up to $5.00, and it's at $5.50, should you go ahead and buy it?

No.

You can go ahead and place a $5.00 Good Til Canceled order—we get into that later

The answer is yes. The stock is under the highest price the newsletter recommends you buy it at.

What if your newsletter recommendation said "Buy Sprint NYSE S up to $5.00." Should you go ahead and buy the stock?

The answer is no.

The analyst that made this newsletter recommendation calculated from their research that your best odds of making money on this stock are if you buy it at $5.00 or below. You are paying for this research. So follow their advice and don't buy the stock now.

Of course, just because the stock is selling for $5.50 right now doesn't mean you can't put an order in for $5.00. And that's what you should do. Place your order at $5.00. I do this all of the time. Because there's a good chance the stock might come down a little into the recommended range in the next few days or weeks. Then you can buy it, and your odds of making a profit are much improved.

But for right now, let's say the recommendation was up to $5.50. The next thing you need to decide is how many shares you are going to buy.

Let's say you have about $500 dollars you want to invest in Sprint. Then you can buy 100 shares which will be a total order of $517 (100 shares X $5.17 per share).

PART 6: Choosing And Buying Good Stocks

Now let's place your order. Click the BUY button and that will take you to a screen that looks something like this.

S Bid: $5.00 Ask: $5.17 Last $5.15					**Review Order**
ACTION	QUANTITY	ORDER TYPE	PRICE	TIME-IN-FORCE	**Place Order**
					Change Order
Buy	10	Limit	$5.17	Day	**Do Not Place**

So what does all of that mean?

Well, you see something that says **Bid $5.00**. That's the price everyone else in the world that wants to buy the stock is willing to pay for it at this moment. But if they put in an order at the price of $5.00 a share, no one will sell it to them.

Why? Because of the next thing you see which says **Ask $5.17**. This is the lowest price anyone in the world that is trying to sell the stock says they will take for it. So if you try to buy it for less than that, probably no one will sell it to you right now, that is.

Finally, you see **Last $5.15**. This tells you how much someone sold the stock for in the last transaction, probably in the past few seconds or minutes. So some of the sellers may be weakening on their price. Remember that these prices are constantly changing – that this is an auction going on. The current price "right this minute" is somewhere between $5.17 (ask) and $5.15 (bid).

You are confident this is a fair price because your newsletter recommendation said to buy up to $5.17.

So you place your order.

Here's how you do that. By the way, there are more refined ways you can buy and we'll discuss a couple of those later, but right now I just want to walk you through the process in a straightforward manner.

In the ACTION box, click the drop down so it says Buy. Don't confuse this with the Buy To Open – that is for stock options, which you are not doing. Just select Buy.

Next enter 10 in the Quantity. This means you want to buy 10 shares of stock.

"Bid" is the price everyone else in the world that wants to buy the stock is willing to pay for it at this moment

"Ask" is the lowest price anyone in the world that wants to sell the stock says they are willing to take for it at this moment

"Ask" is always higher than "Bid" - i.e. the sellers always want to sell for more than the buyers want to pay— go figure

S Bid: $5.00 Ask: $5.17 Last $5.15					Review Order
ACTION	QUANTITY	ORDER TYPE	PRICE	TIME-IN-FORCE	Place Order
					Change Order
Buy	10	Limit	$5.17	Day	Do Not Place

Next make sure the ORDER TYPE says limit. That means you don't want to buy it for more than $5.17, i.e. you are limiting the maximum price you will pay for the stock.

Then enter the price of $5.17 in the PRICE box. This means you want to buy your shares for $5.17 a share or lower.

And then, in the TIME-IN-FORCE box pick Day. That means you want the order to stay in affect all day until the stock is bought. If the stock does not get bought by the end of the day, then the order is canceled.

Now click the Review button and check the display carefully to make sure the order is correct. It should say something like Buy 5 shares of S Sprint at $5.17 a share for a total of $517.00.

Even though you put in a buy price of $5.17, the system will buy it for you lower if the price drops before your order executes ... nice

If the order is not correct, press the Change Order button and make the appropriate changes. Then press the Review Order button one more time to check again. If everything looks okay, press the Place Order button.

Your order just went into the New York Stock Exchange along with millions of other orders from around the world, and the exchange is trying to match your buy order to a sell order so it can buy the stock for you at the price you specified.

For most stocks this will only take a few seconds, minutes at the most, and you will see a screen pop up that says your order has been successfully filled. Congratulations! You just bought your first shares of stock.

Now go back to your Balances and Positions screen and you should see your 10 shares of stock listed. To get to that screen click on the Accounts -- > Balances and Positions tabs and scroll down until you see the stock.

GOOD TIL CANCELED

In the above example, if you wanted to place your order for the Sprint stock at $5.00 a share, even though the market price was $5.17, you could do it by using the good til canceled option in the Time In Force box.

So instead of choosing the Day option, you could choose the GTC (good til canceled) option. The system will set a cancel date about six months in the future instead of at the end of the day with your Day order.

This means any time in the next six months if Sprint goes down to $5.00 or below, your order will automatically be filled at the $5.00 price. And there's a good chance this will happen.

This is making the market come to you on your terms. I do this all the time and my orders get filled quite frequently. And it's free—no charge. So there's no reason not to do this. This is how you win—by setting the situation up so you buy low!

Also, if you don't want the order out there for six months, you can just change the Good Til Canceled Date to something less than six months, like one month or two, or a week. You choose. You're in charge now.

Pretty nice, yes?

PART 7: Protecting Your Stock Investments

Don't Put All Your Eggs In One Basket

Stop Losses

Trailing Stop Losses

Placing A Sell Order

Don't Put All Your Eggs In One Basket

The legendary investor Warren Buffett has two great rules for investing. They are …

Rule 1: Don't lose the money
Rule 2: See Rule Number 1.

This is a huge key to successful investing. So how do we do that? After all, we know that stocks are going to go up and down every day. And going down is losing the money, right.

So here's what we really mean by that. We mean we want to limit (stop) our losses, and let our gains run as far as possible. If we do that right, our losses will be smaller than our gains, and we will make money.

We limit our losses two ways. The first way is not to put all our eggs in one basket. And the second is to literally pick the maximum loss we will accept before we decide to get out of a stock.

Let's start with not putting all our eggs in one basket first.

Putting all of your money in one stock is a big and unnecessary risk, and you could lose it all—like ENRON for example

Never put all of your money in one single stock investment. If you do, you are taking an unnecessary risk and you could lose all of it.

Why? Because none of us can predict the future. And you never know if there will be a headline tomorrow that says something really bad just happened at that company.

Like ENRON, for example. There were people that had their entire retirement investments in this company. Then one day there was a headline that said the management had been cooking the books and reporting profits that were completely made up.

Similarly, never invest in all of the same kinds of stocks. For example, it would not be smart to invest in J. C. Penney's, Macys and Target. Sure, you are invested in more than one stock, but they are all retail department stores.

PART 7: Protecting Your Stock Investments

So what happens to your account when there is a recession and consumers stop spending money? All of your stocks go down — all at once.

So invest in different kinds of stocks. This is known as diversification. You already know there are plenty of different stock recommendations.

So invest in different ones. This is a sign of a good stock investor. And it is a good way to protect your investments.

THE ENRON EGG BASKET

Revealed in October of 2001, the Enron scandal eventually led to the bankruptcy of the Enron Corporation.

This was the largest bankruptcy reorganization in American history at that time. Enron's stock price, which had been as high as $90, plummeted to $1 by the end of November 2001.

So if employees had worked and saved for years and had $90,000 of Enron stock, they had $1000 to show for it at the end of the bankruptcy.

Think about how you would feel if that happened to you. Your hard earned money you invested just vanished.

Remember this if you are tempted to put all your eggs in one basket. While most corporations keep the record keeping straight, someone, somewhere, in some corporation is cooking the books as we speak. Let's hope it's not a corporation we are invested in.

Stop Losses

The other way we keep the money is we "stop" our losses. This activity is actually called setting a stop loss, so that's a new term for you here.

In order to set a stop loss, we actually decide up front when we buy a stock how much we are willing to lose before we throw in the towel and sell it.

This is the best time to do this because we have no money on the table yet, so we are more objective. Let me say that another way. When you have bought a stock, i.e. you have money on the table, it's emotional. The idea here is to get the emotions out of the process before we buy the stock.

So lets talk about stop losses. (Actually, we are going to use something called trailing stop losses, but lets get the stop loss concept down first).

A good stop loss percent to use is 25%. This means if you invested $1000 in a stock, and it went down by $250, so it was worth only $750, you sell it and take the $250 loss.

Why 25% you ask? Well, some credible research and back testing has shown that stop losses in the 21% - 27% range have yielded the most efficient results as far as protecting investments.

$1000

X .25

————

$250

Use a 25% stop loss to protect your investment ...

... because research has shown that a stop loss in the 21%—27% range is the most efficient

Setting the stop losses too thin, say 10%, caused people to stop out of investments too often, only to see them turn around and go higher. And wider stop losses, say 40% to 50%, allowed too much loss before bailing out of a stock in a downward trend.

Simple enough, right? Let me caution you about that. Here's another one of those, "it's simple, but it ain't easy."

Because you will want to hang on to that stock. You will think, well maybe it will come back up to $1000, and I won't lose any money. Every molecule in your body will be screaming to hang on to that stock, and not take the 25% loss

PART 7: Protecting Your Stock Investments

So you watched as your stock went down by 90% … looking back on it you REALLY, REALLY, REALLY wish you had sold when it was ONLY down 25%

Years ago my commodity futures trading partner, Charlie, and I came up with a name for this … we called it the "Hoping-Wishing-Praying" phase … ummm … not a good place to be when investing

Later on Julia Roberts stole that line and made a movie (just kidding)

I know, I know, her movie was actually "Eat Pray Love"

– because you just know it will come back up.

Don't do it. Here's what can happen.

The stock may go on down by 35%. You still have hope so you hang on. Then it's down by 50% -- now you've just got to hang on because you've lost half your money and you want to recover it.

Then it's down 75%, and you are so depressed you don't know what to do. It keeps going down. Now you're down 90% so you think, well, I might as well keep it, I've lost most of my money.

You are correct about part of that. You have lost the money. You broke rule number 1 (rule number 2 also, come to think of it). Looking back on it, you really, really, really wish you had sold it when it was only down 25%, right? That 25% loss doesn't look so bad now.

So don't let this happen to you. Be smart, and if your stock goes down 25%, get out while you still have 75% left.

So those are the basics of stop losses. But we are going to do an even smarter kind of stop loss than I just described. We'll do something called a trailing stop loss. This helps you lose less and even bail out at a profit some times. Read on.

A CAT NAMED KLINGY

When I was a boy, my neighbors had a little black kitten they kiddingly named Klingy. He was a feisty, cool little cat and I used to enjoy walking next door and playing with him.

One morning I went to see him and my neighbor Warren told me Klingy was no longer with us. Klingy had been snoozing in the sun on the front car tire when Warren backed the car out into the street. Apparently, sensing the tire he was sitting on was rolling back and moving down, Klingy had dug his claws in and hung on tight instead of jumping off to safety.

The next time you are tempted to not sell a stock that has dropped below your stop loss limit, I want you to remember Klingy. Because hanging onto a tire rolling down (or a stock) can be hazardous to your (financial) health.

Trailing Stop Losses

Here's an even better way to use stop losses. This technique is called trailing stop losses, and it is what I use.

Instead of just deciding we will sell our stock if it goes down 25% *from where we bought it*, we are going to do something smarter than that.

Whenever the stock goes up higher, we are going to say we will sell it if it goes down 25% from that higher price. So if we bought some shares at $1000, if the stock went down to $750 the next day, we would sell them.

But if the shares went up to $2000, we just made $1000. It's not smart wait until it goes back down to our original $750 stop loss now.

With trailing stops, whenever our stock hits a new high, we set our stop loss standards higher

We set our standards higher. We make our new stop loss 25% from the highest price we've owned it at — $2000. Now we say we will sell the stock if it goes down to $1500.

So in that case, even if the stock goes down 25% from our new stop limit, we sell at a profit. Because we bought the shares at $1000 and we sold them at $1500.

Nice.

If you have just a few stocks you can track and calculate your trailing stop losses manually. You simply keep track of the highest price each stock gets to by writing down the date and price when one of your stocks makes a new high. Then you multiply that by .75 which gives you your new stop loss. Write that down. If your stock goes below that new stop loss price you should sell it.

You have to look at this every day for it to work.

If you have a lot of stocks, you might want to use the Tradestops.com service to automatically adjust the stops higher—and send you an email if it's

Also, you may have wondered why I said multiply the new high price by .75 to get your new trailing stop loss. This is just a shortcut to calculating your new 25% stop loss. For example, if your stock hit a new high of $40 today, you can calculate 25% of it ($40 X .25) which is $10. Then you subtract the $10 from the new high of $40 which gives you your new stop loss of $30.

Or you can just multiply the $40 by .75 which will give you the new stop loss of $30 in one step. It's the same thing, so we do it the easy way.

There are two other ways to do this with much less work. One of them costs a little bit and the other is free (but not as good).

I use a software service called Tradestops to keep track of all of this for me. So whenever I buy a stock, I go to my www.tradestops.com account and enter in the new stock, the price I bought it for, and 25% for the trailing stop percent.

A number of credible financial writers feel it's not a good practice to use stop loss orders—

that is to say orders that automatically sell your stock if it goes below a certain price—

as opposed to just sending you an email notice

Tradestops automatically checks each of my stocks prices every day and moves the trailing top up automatically when they hit a new high price. Then, if my stock goes down 25% below the highest price, it sends me an email alert, and I go to my account and sell the stock.

This is by far the best way to do this. The service costs $9.95 a month, but it is well worth it.

The other way, which is free, is to use this same feature in your trading account. You can put in a "Good Til Canceled" order to sell your stock automatically any time it goes below your 25% trailing stop in the next six month. This is called a stop loss order.

There are two disadvantages to this.

The greatest disadvantage is that the people on the exchanges can see what price you are willing to sell your stock at. With this insider knowledge, in some circumstances, they might be able to manipulate the market price down to your stop loss price temporarily, sell your stock, buy it cheap and then move the market price back up.

If this sounds like cheating – it is. Even though the market is highly regulated and most of the people in the industry are honest, there are always a few bad apples in the bunch. Also, I have no direct proof of this but a number of credible financial writers warn against it.

I think this happens pretty rarely, so your risk is low. But in all my years of trading, I think I have had it happen to me twice. I can't prove that. But the two stocks I am thinking of seemed to move mysteriously down to my stop loss price, get sold, and then quickly pop right back up.

That could have been normal market action ... and then again, maybe not.

When I was a stockbroker, I would routinely enter stop loss orders for clients if they requested it, so it is considered a normal practice by the industry and used frequently. But I thought I'd clue you in on the potential risk.

The other disadvantage is when the stop loss triggers and your stock gets sold. Many experts recommend checking the stock against the stop loss at the end of the trading day, and only then deciding if you will sell it the next day.

This is because the markets may start out high in the morning, move down during the day, then toward the end of the day when the market is about to close, start moving back up. With a stop loss order, you might see your stock get sold at the very bottom during the day, only to watch the price go back up above your stop loss at the end of the day.

So that is a valid consideration.

However, I have found that there is one great advantage to using trailing stop loss orders that automatically sell. That advantage is discipline.

If you feel you just don't have the discipline to sell when you should, that you will just watch your stock go down and hang on to it, hoping, wishing and praying it will go back up instead of selling it like you should, these stop loss orders will do it for you.

On rare and special occasions (beyond the scope of this book) I will use this feature even today because it lets me set up the entire trade beforehand and walk away. I know that if the market hits my predetermined stop, it will just execute my order and be done with it.

The choice is yours. But in general I favor checking at the end of the day and using the Tradestops service to just alert me.

Placing A Sell Order

The process of selling your stock is pretty routine— WHEN to sell is a different story

Even Warren Buffett says he has trouble with that one—so don't feel bad

The process of selling your stock is pretty routine and a lot like buying it.

When to sell your stock is a different story. The most sophisticated investors have trouble with this one, including legendary investor Warren Buffett. So don't feel too bad about yourself if you puzzle over this one.

That said, there are two times when you should sell your stock.

One is when it hits your 25% trailing stop. So you sell in this case to limit your losses. The other time is the happier occasion when you have made money and want to take your profits.

So let's say a few months have gone by and your Sprint stock, which you bought for $5.17 a share, is now going for $10.00 a share.

Wow. Nice profit. So you decide to sell your 10 shares for $10 a share. You bought them for a total of $517. And you are going to sell them for $1000. That's a happy story.

To do this, log in to your stock account and then click on the Accounts —> Balances and Positions tabs. Look for the Sprint stock and it's symbol, carefully noting how many shares you own (which is 10 in this example).

You can do this by clicking on the stock directly on that screen, or you can click on Research and Ideas —> Stocks tabs and enter the symbol S in the box.

Either way will get you to the screen that shows the current value of the stock. Remember, this is exactly the same screen you went to when you were getting ready to buy the stock.

You will see something like the screen that follows. This screen should look familiar. So what does this tell us?

First, that we got the right stock (Sprint). This is the one we want to sell. And second, that the stock's value is now $10.00 a share.

That's all we need to know. So now we click the Sell button. That will bring us to a screen like this one.

S Bid: $10.00 Ask: $10.17 Last $10.00					Review Order
					Place Order
ACTION	QUANTITY	ORDER TYPE	PRICE	TIME-IN-FORCE	**Change Order**
Sell	10	Limit	$10.00	Day	**Do Not Place**

So what does all of that mean?

Well, you see something that says Bid $10.00. That's the price everyone else in the world that wants to buy the stock is willing to pay for it at this moment.

The next thing you see says Ask $10.17. This is the lowest price anyone in the world that is trying to sell the stock is asking for it. But you've already decided on $10.00, and that's what people are willing to pay, so no matter.

Finally, you see Last at $10.00. This tells you how much someone sold the stock for in the last transaction, probably in the past seconds or minutes. That works out just fine. That's what you are going to sell for.

Remember that these prices are constantly changing – that this is an auction going on. The current price "right this minute" is $10.00.

So you get ready to sell by filling in the boxes.

PART 7: Protecting Your Stock Investments

					Review Order
S Bid: $10.00 Ask: $10.17 Last $10.00					Review Order
					Place Order
ACTION	QUANTITY	ORDER TYPE	PRICE	TIME-IN-FORCE	Change Order
Sell	10	Limit	$10.00	Day	Do Not Place

Here's how you do that.

Make sure the ACTION BOX says Sell. Do not chose Sell To Close. That is for stock options. Just use Sell.

Enter 10 in the quantity. That's the number of shares you are going to sell.

You're probably tired of me warning you about accidently putting on a short sale at this point— so I promise this is the last time—just don't sell more shares than you own

CAUTION! Make sure you DO NOT accidently enter more shares than you own. Be very careful with this box when you are selling. If you enter more shares than you own, you have created a "short sale." This can create an unlimited liability for you. By that I mean you could lose much more than your investment. Theoretically it could be a huge loss – think more like losing your house, car, etc.

Next make sure the ORDER TYPE says limit. That means you don't want to sell for less than $10.00 a share, i.e. you are limiting the downside on the price.

Then enter the price of $10.00 in the PRICE box. This means you want to sell your shares at $10.00 a share (or better). And then in the TIME-IN-FORCE box pick Day.

This means you want the order to stay in affect all day until the stock sells. If the stock does not sell by the end of the day then the order is canceled.

Now click the Review button and check the display carefully to make sure the order is correct. It should say something like Sell 10 shares of S Sprint at $10.00 a share for a total of $1000.00.

If the order is not correct, press the Change Order button and make the appropriate changes.

Then press the Review Order button one more time to check again. If everything looks okay, press the Place Order

PART 7: Protecting Your Stock Investments

S Bid: $10.00 Ask: $10.17 Last $10.00					Review Order
ACTION	QUANTITY	ORDER TYPE	PRICE	TIME-IN-FORCE	Place Order
					Change Order
Sell	10	Limit	$10.00	Day	Do Not Place

Your sell order just went out to the New York Stock Exchange along with millions of other orders and the exchange is trying to match your sell order to a buy order so it can sell the stock for you at the price you specified (or better).

For most stocks this will only take a few seconds, minutes at the most, and you will see a screen pop up that says your order has been successfully filled.

Congratulations! You just sold your first shares of stock.

Now go back to your Balances and Positions screen and you should see that your 10 shares of stock are no longer listed. You will also see where your cash total just went up by $1000.

Nice.

PART 8: Summary And Conclusion

Checking On Your Stocks Day To Day

Final Thoughts And Reminders

Next Steps

About The Author

PART 8: Summary And Conclusion

Checking On Your Stocks Day To Day

You'll probably want to check on your stocks at least once a day

You will probably want to check on your stocks at least once a day.

This is not absolutely necessary if you have the stop loss alerts set up as I mentioned in earlier chapters. However, most people are curious about how the market is treating them. I check on mine multiple times a day because I find it interesting.

Here's how you do this is with your Discount Broker account.

Simply log on and then click the tabs **Accounts —> Balances & Positions**.

This will show you the total value of your account at this moment. If you click the refresh symbol, you will see that the value probably changed up or down.

It changed in the few seconds since the last time you clicked. This is because the value of all your stocks is changing second by second. And the system is constantly updating the prices and recalculating the value of all of your individual stocks and the total value of your account.

Some people, (and I won't mention his name), have been known to click the refresh button repeatedly to see how their stocks are going up and down, second by second

I have been known to click the refresh button repeatedly a number of times just to see how my account is going up and down, second by second, but I'm sure you won't ever do that ;-).

Remember, stocks are traded at big auctions (known as exchanges, like the New York Stock Exchange), so their value changes constantly as people bid more or less for the stocks.

And they are trading on those stocks from all around the world. You are truly participating in a global activity.

If you scroll down on the screen you will see how each stock you own is doing at the moment. This is also very interesting.

For example, here is a stock I was invested in as I was writing this chapter.

PART 8: Summary And Conclusion

Symbol	Description	Qty	Purchase Price	Cost	Market Value	Gain($)	Day Gain($)
MOO	MARKET VECTORS AGRIBUSINESS	100	50	5000	6000	1000	100

I owned a Market Vectors Agricultural investment during this writing — so of course the market symbol for that was MOO ... these guys are not without a sense of humor.

This is an agricultural investment, so of course the symbol for it is MOO (these guys aren't without a sense of humor).

QTY shows that I own 100 shares.

Purchase Price shows I paid $50 for each share.

Cost shows that I paid $5000 in total. Makes sense, right? I own 100 shares and they cost $50 each.

Market Value says my 100 shares are worth $6000 right now.

Gain Dollars shows how much money I have made since I bought them. Makes sense, right? I paid $5000 for them and they are worth $6000 now.

Day Gain $ shows I've lost $100 on them today. So that means they must have been worth $6100 yesterday and today they are down $100.

But that's not a big worry to me. Why?

Because stocks go up and stocks go down but I've still made $1000 since I bought them. They may go back up $100 yet today. Or tomorrow.

Remember, by using trailing stops, I only start getting worried when they are down 25% from the best price I ever owned them. If that is $6100, they would have to go down by $1525. They are nowhere close to that. So I don't worry about it.

So that's about it on checking up on your stocks. I think once you start doing it you'll find it quite interesting.

And you might discover you are one of those people that keeps hitting the refresh button repeatedly. Like somebody else I know, whose name we won't mention.

PART 8: Summary And Conclusion

Final Thoughts And Reminders

So we've come down a fair path together, you and I ...

So we've come down a fair path together, you and I. By now you know the basics of what it takes to be a good stock investor.

Let's briefly review the concepts and steps one last time.

- As a stock investor you are a business owner. No smart business person would buy a business without good research.

- Subscribe to at least one newsletter, read the research and decide on which stock(s) to buy.

- When you buy, get your Warren Buffett billionaire mindset on and do not pay one penny more than the recommended price. Make the market come to you.

- Don't put all of your eggs in one basket. Buy different kinds of stocks. Remember ENRON.

- Protect your stocks with trailing stops.

- ALWAYS sell a stock if it goes below your trailing stop. Remember what happened to Klingy the cat.

- Check on your stocks at least once a day, and write down any of them that hit new highs. Calculate your new trailing stop by multiplying that number by .75.

- Remember that buying stocks cheap and on sale greatly increases you odds of success and reduces your risk.

- Keep some cash in your account to buy stocks cheap when the market is down — only amateurs are always fully invested.

- Have fun with it and be proud. You are a special person that has chosen to take charge of your financial life.

That's it. Just ten simple rules. But you must do every single one of them. If you do them all you are a responsible investor. If you do not, you are a gambler.

PART 8: Summary And Conclusion

Next Steps

So how did you do? I bet you did just fine. With a few basics and a simple method, you can do this, can't you? So what are your next steps?

Well, first I would suggest you just keep following the **Stock Market For Beginners** method you've just read, day by day, until you feel comfortable with it and it starts to be routine. This is a solid approach to improving your odds with the stock market – if you follow ALL of the steps and don't take shortcuts.

That said, of course, there are advanced techniques beyond the Stock Market For Beginners that can lead you to even greater success.

Like a simple, free way to get many of your stock picks at a discount.

- *You won't believe how easy this one is. And it's free to do. It costs you no more to buy your stocks this way than how you buy them today.*

- *I use this method frequently and continue to be surprised how often it works. I call it my EXTREME Warren Buffett attitude.*

- *And of course you need to know the technique.*

Or a way to make even more money with the stocks you already own.

- *Most people don't know about this one.*

- *But I've got to tell you, if you aren't doing this you are throwing money away.*

- *I use this technique frequently to boost my profits.*

If these interest you, then you'll find them in the next book in the series called *Beyond* **Stock Market For Beginners.**

In Beyond Stock Market For Beginners, we learn an advanced technique to make even more money with stocks you already own

I've got to tell you ... if you aren't doing this you are just throwing money away

So if you want to learn about them and take stock investing to the next level, be sure and order the *Beyond* **Stock Market For Beginners** book, written in the same easy to understand style.

I've enjoyed working with you in ***Stock Market For Beginners.***

See you in *Beyond* **Stock Market For Beginners.**

To your health and prosperity,

John Roberts

P.S. I always love to hear your comments and suggestions. So be sure and send them on to me in an email at JohnRoberts@LiveLearnAndProsper.com. Just put Stock Market in the subject line. I read all of my emails.

P.P.S. As a buyer of **Stock Market For Beginners**, you are entitled to sign up for the free Live, Learn And Prosper newsletter (a $27.00 value).

You'll get more tips, thoughts and techniques coming your way about every week or two. You can sign up here at www.LiveLearnAndProsper.com. Did I mention this is free?

PART 8: Summary And Conclusion

About The Author ... John Roberts

"It's not the years in your life that count, but the life in your years"

John is the Founder and CEO of Live Learn And Prosper.com, a leading newsletter and website where informed living meets success. His books and articles are known for their easy to understand writing style explaining complex things.

He's been a life-long investor and prior to founding LLAP, was a Financial Consultant and Stockbroker (formerly licensed with the New York Stock Exchange) and Senior Business Analyst. Before that, he managed the Corporate IT Department of a Fortune 500 Corporation, and earlier in his career, he served as the Senior Programmer/Designer for May Department Stores International, spending time in London, England designing and programming a large scale international foreign buying system. He also served in the United States Marine Corps.

But all is not work and investments in John's life. Called a renaissance man by his friends, he is also an award winning photographer, cartoonist, published author and avid sailor, believing that life should be an adventure.

He recalls one Thanksgiving finding himself singlehandedly sailing his boat the ***Saline Solution*** in the Florida Keys — on the far edge of tropical storm Keith. He says when he finally made it back safely to port, it was the most thankful Thanksgiving of his life. He also allows this may have been a bit too much adventure.

John's had a life long commitment to self-improvement and achieving goals — for himself and teaching others. He had an early start in life achieving higher goals as a "lettered" fiberglass pole-vaulter in high school, clearing 12' when the world record was 17'. And still earlier, as a big brother teaching his younger twin sisters how to read before kindergarten.

John currently resides in Miami, Orlando or St. Louis — depending on when you ask him. When he's not too busy writing in Florida you can often find him sailing or soaking up sun at the beach.

Thanks for buying Stock Market For Beginners.

Could you do me a favor and tell me what you thought of it, so I can write even better things for you in the future? I know you are busy, so just six little questions …

1) Did the book help you understand stock investing?
   No _____   A little _____   Some _____   Quite a bit _____   A lot _____

2) Would you recommend it to a friend?   __ Yes   __ No

3) What are some things you liked about it?

   _____

   _____

4) What could I have done better? Don't hold back here—I asked for it :-).

   _____

   _____

   _____

5) How much did you know about the stock market before reading this book?
   Not much _____   A little _____   Some _____   Quite a bit _____   A lot _____

6) Would you be willing to write your name and a testimonial below that I could use. **I protect your privacy by just using an initial and name, like J. Smith or Jane S.**

   _____

   _____

   _____

Continue on the next page if you need room. You may email your thoughts and responses directly to me at John Roberts@ LiveLearnAndProsper.com or mail to John Roberts; 3123 S. Semoran Blvd Suite 289; Orlando, FL 32822.

And thank you for your time and feedback.

To your health and prosperity—John Roberts

Made in the USA
Columbia, SC
15 February 2025